Global Dimensions

Focus on Contemporary Issues (FOCI) addresses the pressing problems, ideas and debates of the new millennium. Subjects are drawn from the arts, sciences and humanities, and are linked by the impact they have had or are having on contemporary culture. FOCI books are intended for an intelligent, alert audience with a general understanding of, and curiosity about, the intellectual debates shaping culture today. Instead of easing readers into a comfortable awareness of particular fields, these books are combative. They offer points of view, take sides and are written with passion.

SERIES EDITORS
Barrie Bullen and Peter Hamilton

In the same series

Cool Rules
Dick Pountain and David Robins

Chromophobia
David Batchelor

Celebrity
Chris Rojek

Global Dimensions
Space, Place and the Contemporary World

JOHN RENNIE SHORT

REAKTION BOOKS

For Lisa

Published by Reaktion Books Ltd
79 Farringdon Road
London EC1M 3JU, UK

www.reaktionbooks.co.uk

First published 2001

Copyright © John Rennie Short, 2001

All rights reserved
No part of this publication may be reproduced, stored in a
retrieval system, or transmitted, in any form or by any means,
electronic, mechanical, photocopying, recording or otherwise,
without the prior permission of the publishers.

Designed by Libanus Press
Printed and bound by Biddles Limited, Guildford and King's Lynn

British Library Cataloguing in Publishing Data
Short, John R. (John Rennie), 1951–
  Global dimensions: space, place and the contemporary world. – (FOCI)
  1. Globalization
  I. Title
  337

ISBN 1 86189 102 4

Contents

1 The Dialectics of Globalization　7
2 What Time is this Place?　21
3 Does a Global Polity Mean the End of the Nation–State?　51
4 A Global Economy?　87
5 Global Cultures　115
6 Border Spaces　135
7 The Annihilation of Space, the Tyranny of Time　159
8 Democratizing Globalization　179
References　185
Select Bibliography　187
Acknowledgements　189
List of Illustrations　190

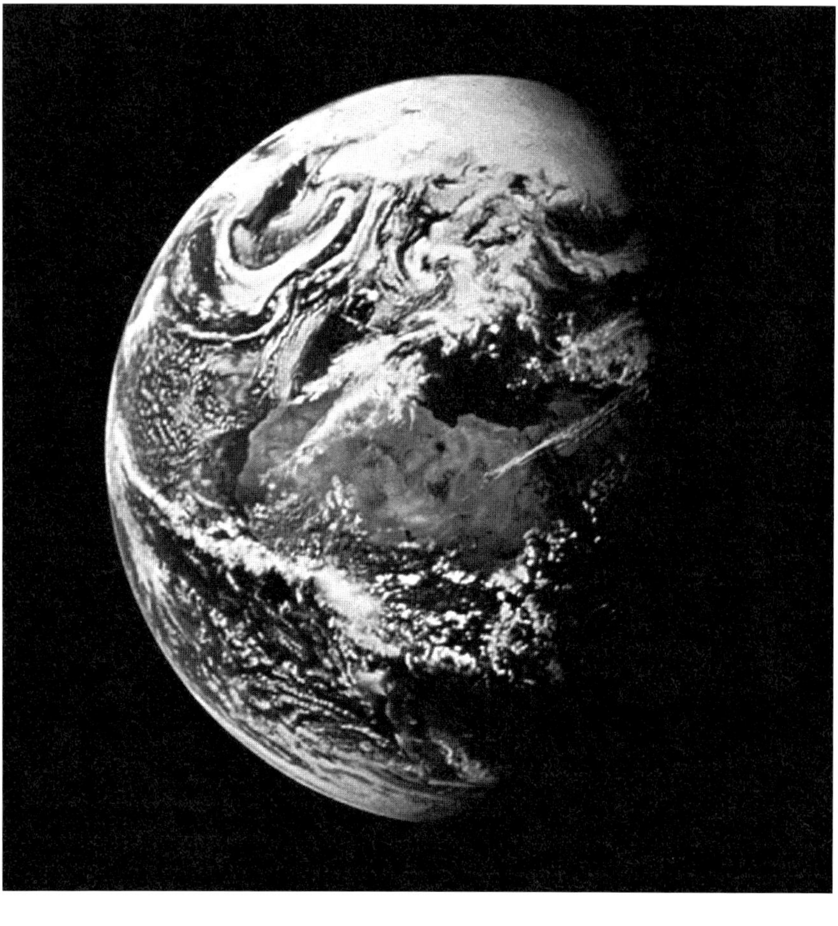

CHAPTER ONE

The Dialectics of Globalization

Globalization. Something new, or the same old thing? A process impossible to control, or something that needs be managed? A corporate conspiracy (a con trick pulled by the rich and powerful), or a brave new world, pregnant with emancipatory opportunities?

Rarely has a word evoked such feeling. *Globalization* is one of those terms that has made its way from somewhere inside the academy to circulate in the public realm of commentaries, newspapers reports, TV documentaries, political speeches and public discussions. And, like all escapees, it has taken on a variety of disguises. It represents different things to a factory worker, a merchant banker, a shanty-town dweller, a suburbanite, someone in China, a Detroit resident. The word has come to mean and represent different things and to evoke a variety of responses. A word often used to describe homogeneity has heterogeneous meanings and diverse interpretations.

Globalization has become one of the most powerful and persuasive ideas to have captured the collective imagination, sometimes as dream, sometimes as nightmare. It is used in the popular press, in magazines and in news reports as a sort of shorthand way of saying that the world is becoming more alike. The business press, in particular, promotes the notion that we are moving towards a fully integrated global economy. It is also used as a marketing concept to sell goods, commodities and services. *Going global* has become the mantra for a whole range of companies, business gurus and institutions eager to position themselves in a new economic order. Globalization has also become a term of criticism. Forms of globaphobia are found around the world; at the extreme it is often tied to conspiratorial theories of a new world order imposed by a cabal of the rich and connected. There is a growing anxiety with what globalization represents: unwanted change, the foreign other, an incomprehensible force that is beyond national, let alone individual, control. Globalization has also become the subject of an expanding academic debate – witness the growing number of books, articles, conferences and even professional careers devoted to it.

Globalization commentators come in all stripes, from the avowed globalists who see the death of the nation–state to sceptics who see globalization as more myth than reality, a sort of intellectual confidence trick that generalizes from a few case studies. My own view is that of a sceptical globalist. Globalization has increased in intensity and impact, but it is generating difference as well as similarity. It comes with risks, but also with opportunities. Corporate power is globalized, but so are social movements.

When I told friends I was writing a book on globalization, they asked, 'Isn't everyone?' There are many works on the subject. Many assume that globalization is a recency. I argue, in contrast, that its present round has deep historical roots. Globalization is often presented as a sort of tidal wave sweeping away local distinctiveness. In that scenario, it is a tsunami of change that is wiping out the uniqueness of localities, an alien force washing away local differences. My argument is that the contemporary world is not a pre-global state awaiting the global storm. I contend that there have a been a series of pronounced globalizations since *c.* 1500, and especially since 1870. The world is composed of places with different histories and geographies of reglobalizations.

In this book I also explore the way that globalization unfolds over space. Conventional opinion sees globalization as making everywhere the same. I will argue that at the heart of globalization is an ambiguity: I will show that globalization is making places both different and the same. It is bringing peoples closer apart and places further together.

There is a spatial dialectic to globalization. On the one hand, some places have moved closer together in relative space. The trajectories of national, regional and local economies have become even more enmeshed within a network of global financial flows and transactions. But on the other hand, some places, subject to a process of financial exclusion, have moved further apart in relative space, and this has led to a widening of economic and social spaces between such 'places of exclusion' and those that are heavily interrelated in terms of the global economic system. Some of the most global cities have low-income areas that are starved of resources and are disconnected from the circuits of globalization. There is a new geography of global centrality and peripheralization that cuts across national boundaries.

With increasing economic competition and capital mobility, the outcome is often increasingly uneven development and spatial differentiation rather than homogenization. The world is becoming more interconnected, but the world is not necessarily becoming more alike.

The rapid capital flows, the decline of transport costs and the rise of electronic communication have prompted some analysts to write of the end of geography. But in a competitive world, the small differences in relative space become even more important. Whether it is in location relative to markets, or perceived quality of life, quality of environment, variations in wage rates or systems of regulation and local business culture, characteristics of place take on crucial significance. The friction of distance has not yet become the fiction of distance. Against a background of a shrinking world, geography has become more important, not less.

Much of the literature on globalization has a curiously ahistorical, aspatial approach. It is presented as a condition devoid of real history and substantive geography. We should avoid such simple representations about the contemporary world. We need to examine critically the notion of globalization through a geographical framing of globalization. Space and place are central to how globalization is constituted. Globalization is not an untethered phenomenon, it is grounded in time and space.

Defining Globalization

Globalization is a process that links people and places, institutions and events around the world. As a shorthand definition we can say that globalization is the increasing tendency for the world to be a single network of flows of money, ideas, people and things. It is the world-wide distribution and interaction of economic, political and cultural processes. But these processes create difference within circuits of connection.

There are three processes by which places are shaped by globalization: economic, political and cultural. It is often assumed that the end state of these processes entails a global economy, a global polity and a global culture.

Our global economy has been maturing for some 500 years. Worldwide flows of capital and labour have been connecting places and integrating them into the world economy since the sixteenth century. The speed, intensity, amount and reach of capital flows have been truly ubiquitous since the 1970s. Globalization is a compression of the world by these flows – flows that are broadening as well as deepening. They have brought about a greater degree of interdependence. Global markets in finance, trade and services now operate through a regulatory umbrella that is not so much state-centred as market-centred. Capital now has more extensive rights than at any time in history, and capitalists now operate throughout a more extensive and intensive global grid.

A global polity has become more of a possibility with the decline of the Soviet bloc. International organizations are increasingly important, while regimes of security, trade and human rights have become far more prominent in organizing political space. For instance, the international human rights regime provides a political and legal framework for promoting a universal conception of individual rights. However, despite the new forms for political spatial organization, the nation–state has shown a tremendous resilience. Those announcements of the death of the nation–state are premature. The real question is not whether the state is being replaced, but how the nation–state is responding to the new geopolitico-economic realities.

Cultural globalization, as compared to economic and political versions, is a far more difficult arena to distinguish. Progress in economic globalization has contributed to cultural globalization. The globalization of culture proceeds through the continuous flow of ideas, information, commitment, values and tastes across the world, mediated via mobile individuals, signs, symbols and electronic simulations.[1] While the same images and commodities are found around the world, they are interpreted, consumed and used in different ways. The great challenge is to understand the complex interaction between culture and the consumption of ideas, signs and material goods. The heart of a culture involves attachment to place, language, religion, values, tradition and customs. Drinking Coca-Cola does not make Russians think like Americans any more than eating sushi makes the British more like the Japanese. Throughout human history, fashions and material goods have diffused from one cultural realm to another. However, we do need to acknowledge that the channels for cultural mixing are now more open than ever before. But rather than a single unitary global culture, it is more accurate to speak of a variety of global cultures.

The three processes of economic, political and cultural globalization vary in intensity and depth around the world, and can exhibit idiosyncratic interfaces with local phenomena. Cultural globalization does not necessarily follow from economic globalization. In any one place in the world, the precise mix of these three processes produces a marked difference with all other parts of the world. The same, yet differentiated is a more accurate way to describe the results of globalization.

I will examine the dialectic in each of these sets of processes. Economic globalization is joining up the world in a series of economic transactions, but, in doing so, it is making the world different; it is, for example, exacerbating differences between *global* cities and rural hinterlands situated within the same country as those global cities. Sydney, for example, is becoming more like Los Angeles, but less like parts of Australia's Outback. Political globalization is the move towards a global polity, yet there has been a renationalization of the state, as national boundaries become more porous for some transactions but constitute higher walls for others. Some states are both coming together and pulling apart. Cultural globalization is not making us more alike, but both more alike and different at the same time. There is now similar material being consumed in different ways across the world.

A Question of Scale

Globalization can be compared with localism and nationalism. If all my relatives and friends, ideas, goods and services come from the area or region in which I live, then I am living a local life. My society is localized rather than globalized. If my gods dwell in the local forests, the regional flora and fauna meet my material needs, and my culture, including my language, is singular and particular, then I live in a local world. There are few examples left today of local cultures of this kind.

The local is not separated out from the national. Our local communities are regulated by the national. Our local everyday lives are suffused with the national. When I buy something in a local store in America, I am using money printed by a central authority in a transaction regulated by State and Federal legislation.

The local is not separated out from the global either. I look around at my own world shaped by local, national and global considerations. Born into a large working-class family in a small village in Scotland, I went to graduate school and employment in England. I now live in the United States. My extended family is just that – one that is extended across the world. I drive cars designed in Japan for a global market, but made in the US and advertised by a self-consciously Australian film actor. My clothes are made in Costa Rica, Italy, Honduras, Indonesia. One of my suits was designed by Italians, made in Yugoslavia from Australian wool and sold by a Swedish company with outlets across Europe and North America. The level of global consumption has grown in recent years, but throughout most of my life, even when I had less disposable income and more modest consumption patterns, the global has impinged on my local. My family was deeply affected by two World Wars and the intervening Great Depression. My father fought in the Korean War. The family's economic fortunes were always tied to the global economy. There were two main sources of work in my Scots community: woollen mills employing women, and coalmines for the men. A global shift in textiles manufacturing and changes in the relative price of coal on the world market has dried up these two sources of employment. Engineering factories in nearby towns also went under in the wake of the global shift of manufacturing and the resultant de-industrialization of the local economy. While these details are particular, the broad sequence of events is not. They have happened almost everywhere in the world over the past 100 years. The local has been shaped by the global.

It is tempting to see history as a steady progression from the local through the national to the global. The global then becomes an end-point of a process of increasing scale, intensity and velocity of flows that began local and are now global. A technological basis for this shift is often promoted. When the train replaced the cart and was then, in turn, replaced by the aircraft as the dominant mode of transportation, the range of possible interaction moved from the local to the global. There is a element of truth in this. But consider. The global is not recent, and connections between local, national and global are older and more complex than this simplified model would suggest. Even the constraints of travelling on foot did not stop Alexander the Great's army from reaching India. We have always lived in a world in which there have been flows of people, ideas, goods and services beyond the local. To be sure, some have been more global than others, but globalization, like localism and nationalism, has been a central feature of social–spatial organization for at least 500 years. Maybe much, much longer. How about 30,000 years? That is how long *Homo sapiens* as a species has occupied much of the habitable world. A case can be made that we have always lived in a single world. From the same roots and a single source, we have, as a species, diffused globally. If we adopt this grander perspective, we recognize the historically limited view that explains us as initially separated, and only recently coming together. History has for too long been written in tribal and, in turn, in national terms, full of folk memories and regional tales. We need a more cosmopolitan perspective in order to see that the one compelling historical narrative is that of a single world.

A more critical view of globalization would acknowledge a more complex relationship between the three scales – global, national and local. The local is not simply a passive recipient of global processes. Processes flow from the local to the global as much as from the global to the local; good examples are the growth in ethnic cuisines throughout the world and the blendings that make hybrid cuisines.

Understanding globalization is only possible if we give greater attention to the appropriate scale of analysis and develop a more profound sense of the causal links that connect each of the scales. We also need to understand the changes in meaning of each of these terms. Local, national and global have themselves always been changing, unstable categories.

Space, Place and the Geographical Fix

Space and place. These two words – both simple, but packed with meaning – are central to my analysis. There is a commonsense feeling that space is more general while place is more particular. *Space* has a number of meanings: as a noun it means the interval between things; as a verb, *to space* implies putting in some sort of order. *Place*, in contrast is personalized space, occupied space. To know your place, to be put into place, is to be situated in a definite location. There are both sentiment and power associations behind these phrases. Space is a background, a container, but when transformed into a certain place, it is not neutral to the pulse of power. The transformation of space into place through demarcation, exclusion and containment are all embodiments of how and why power is wielded. Spatial transgression and contestation are examples of resistance. There is a geography of power as well as power in geography. Place can be used to define and exclude. Place is my space, our space. But your place can often be seen as simply empty space. Space and place are vital to individual and group identity. Space and place are what make me and you, us and them.

Space and place are connected to each other. The following table lists only some of the other notions intertwined with the space/place division:

SPACE	PLACE
them	us
there	here
general	particular

motion	rest
universal	vernacular
global	local
Apollo	Dionysus
modern	postmodern
global village	village in the city
mind	body
becoming	being
spirit	soul

Place is space that is occupied. The identity of self, group and nation is bound up with ideas and representations of particular space. Even the most general term – human – implies, this side of intergalactic travel at least, occupancy on one place, the earth. The more detailed the definitions of identity, the more they are associated with particular places. The difference between us and them is often based on location. We come from here, they are from there. What makes it *there* is them and what makes it *here* is us.

Nietzsche made a big deal of the difference between being and becoming. It is legitimate to suggest the notion of here and there as equally central elements to the human condition. It is becoming all the more interesting when the connection between identity and location is not so fixed. When Melbourne is the third largest 'Greek' city, or there are more Scots living outside of Scotland than within it, what does it mean to be an Australian Greek or a Scots American? Does it mean cultural identity is being de-territorialized, losing that place connection, or re-territorialized with hybrid identities undermining and reinforcing the relationship between identity and space? Or some combination?

Space and place are human practices as well as linguistic turns. And yet, many of the spatial categories that we use in public speech have become strangely untethered from the world. Sexuality, identity, the market are all words that can lose their sense of space and place. The market, for example, was first an actual place where goods were traded. Now the term is used as a sort of generic notation in the press, a set of equations in neo-classical economics; it has become a spatial fiction. In the shift from place to metaphor to fiction, we lose the sense of site and location, setting and context. Words and ideas can become ways out of our earthbound existence rather than depictions of our tethered condition.

Space and place are under-theorized. We owe much to the nineteenth century, the century of Marx and Darwin. These two thinkers, in their different ways, prioritized time over space and both of these over any conception of place. They wrote about evolution, change (social and biological) and historical inevitability, yet they said little about space and place. They, like many others, saw a world in the process of becoming rather than being; social life as a series of stages rather than as a set of locations. We are still infected by their virus of temporal prioritization, which lauded progress over tradition, society in the process of becoming, over community that was tethered in time and place. They celebrated time rather than space. The solidification of these place-transcending ideologies of Progress and Evolution continues. Globalism has replaced Modernization, which, in turn, displaced Progress as the new aspatial non-place meta-narrative.

Locations constitute both space and place. Locations are a geographical fix of economic, political and cultural processes at the local, national and global scales. These scalar processes create space and generate place. This fix is never static or completed; locations are always in the process of becoming. The processes of globalization flow into and out of this place–space nexus in a variety of ways. The popular view is that globalization leads to space. The particularities of place are overwhelmed by globalization to create a bland space that covers most of the world. I contend that globalization is a dialectic process that creates both space and place. The connection between location and globalization is not simply the creation of space; it is the formation of new forms of a space–place nexus. Globalization unfolds over space; globalization takes place. Through and in globalization place is transformed into space and space is reworked into place.

The very definitions of space and place have been unstable categories, and this instability, rather than showing a conceptual fuzziness, represents the way our depiction of the world, our spatial awareness and our place sensitivity has shifted and changed as material practices transformed how we see the world and our place in it. In the construction of space, for example, there has been a shift from absolute to relative conceptions, brought about by the success of a globalization. The creation of absolute space has led to the emergence of conceptions of relative space. It is not so important where you are as it is when you are. In the world of ideas, for example, there has been a shift in recent years from the subjects listed in the right-hand column to the left-hand one in my Space–Place table. This shift, sometimes dramatic, but often barely perceptible, has been given a number of names, the best-known one being *postmodern turn*. The paradox is that while there has been a shift from right to left in economic transactions, there has been a shift from left to right in intellectual practice. In cultural matters, we have shifted from space to place, while in economic concerns, we have moved from place to space.

The spatial dialectic of globalization is the construction of space and the creation of place. Globalization constructs space through space–time convergence, cultural homogenization, economic reglobalization and political (dis)integration. But the same things are also creating places. Nationalism, community consciousness and the self-conscious construction of ethnic identity are as much a part of globalization as 24-hour markets and global travel. The self-same forces not only connect, they differentiate the world. The world is becoming more interconnected and more different.

Space and place are being reconstructed and reproduced in new and fascinating ways. A popular view is that the world is becoming more the same; space is reigning supreme as globalism becomes the ruling *Zeitgeist* of the day. My opinion is that the world is becoming increasingly different precisely because the differential impact of these spatial waves of similarity are creating places of difference. Globalism is both creating and undermining the construction of place. This book, in essence, is this last sentence extended and nuanced. To understand the spaces of globalization and the globalization of place, we need to explore the complex relationships between globalization, space and place. I will show that globalization is bringing peoples closer apart and places further together.

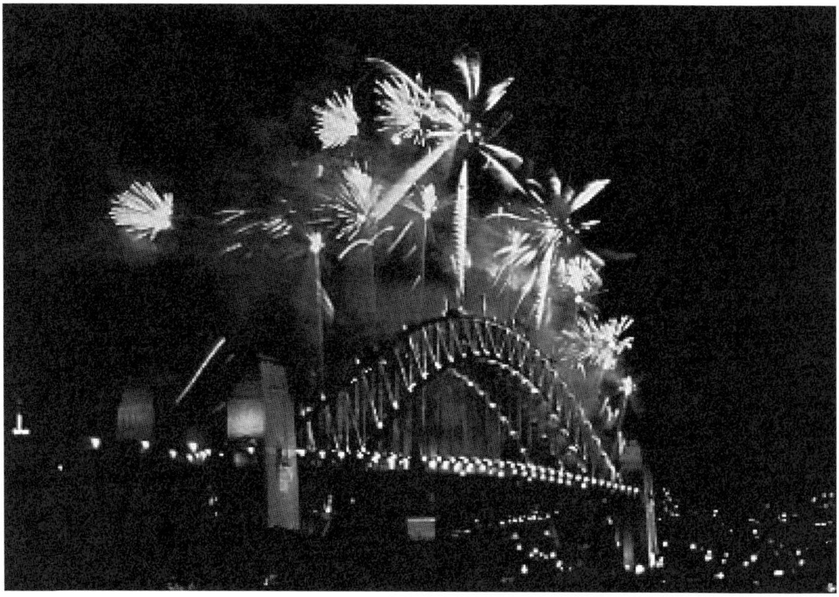

CHAPTER TWO

What Time is this Place?

1884? All dates are arbitrary. But some are less arbitrary than others. This date marks the beginnings of a global metric of space–time. The first International Meridian Conference opened in Washington, DC, in 1884.

The world is a giant clock that turns continually on its own axis as well as moving around the sun. If we measure time by when the sun is highest in the sky, then different places in the world will always have different times from one another. Until recently there were a variety of local times. In Britain, Oxford was around eight minutes behind London. When you could only walk or ride or take a boat from the capital up the Thames to Oxford, the difference was negligible. But with the coming of the railways all that changed. Local time was now an inconvenience. The particularities of place were being overwhelmed by a new form of travel that collapsed space–time. The coming of the railways brought places closer together. It shrank the time taken to travel between places and rendered awkward the proliferation of local times. In 1883 the railways in the US instituted Standard Time, which replaced local times with uniform time zones. Place had been turned into space.

The measuring grid of space, at least since the Renaissance, has been latitude and longitude. The world is imagined as a mesh. Lines of latitude run east to west parallel to the equator and the location of any place can be fixed with reference to how far north or south from the equator it is. Lines of longitude run north and south and allow locations to be fixed east or west of a prime meridian. However, there is no obvious line of longitude that can be predetermined as the prime meridian. One line of longitude is much like another; there is no natural prime meridian. Classical scholars, who started to grid the world almost 2,000 years ago, used a variety of prime meridians: Hipparchos chose Rhodes, while both Ptolemy and Marinus preferred the Canary Islands.

From the Renaissance to 1884 a variety of prime meridians were in place. The French, Dutch, Belgians and Portuguese each used their capital cities. The British opted for Greenwich on the south-east edge of London, although after the American Revolution, mapmakers in the new-founded USA changed their prime meridian from Greenwich to Philadelphia (the capital from 1790–1800) and then to Washington, DC. Throughout the nineteenth century many American maps employed a double system on the same page, with longitude from Washington, DC, at the bottom and Greenwich at the top.

In 1871 an International Congress met in Antwerp and agreed that sea charts needed a standard prime meridian. It was to become obligatory within fifteen years. Progress had been made by the early 1880s: most countries adopted the new system, although the French still used Paris, the Spanish Cadiz and the Portuguese Lisbon. The Brazilians used both Greenwich and Rio de Janerio, while the Swedes, always polite and accommodating, used Greenwich and Paris as well as Stockholm. At the second International Geographical Conference in Rome in 1875, it was agreed to use Greenwich as the prime meridian on land maps, although it was hoped that this honour would encourage Britain to adopt the metric system. (Britain proved recalcitrant on this matter, however, and feet and yards, stones and pounds, pints and quarts were to last well into the next century.) But the world now had a global metric: local time had been replaced by a standard time centred on the Observatory at Greenwich. Space had triumphed over place.

A Global Celebration

The new temporal metric allowed the internationalization of events. The global metric allowed global celebrations. Fast forward 116 years to 1 January 2000. With an agreed-on calendar and space–time grid, the world could enjoy a 24-hour celebration of what many considered the dawn of the new millennium. At 1000 Greenwich Mean Time, first up was Kiribati in the Pacific. This republic of 33 islands of coral sand and rock fragments that 85,000 people call home, was the first country to see in the new millennium. Three years earlier, Kiribati, in preparation for the event, had the date-line moved to follow its eastern border. It also joined the UN in September 1999, just in time to be part of the international community before the big day. Kiribati wanted the honour and media attention of being the first nation into the new millennium. Above the celebrations, a Scots couple, John and Marion Deans, jumped from an aeroplane in order to see the new day from 12,000 feet above Millennium Island.

I was fixed to my TV during many of these events. Not all the time. But at a few minutes to each hour, I would tune in to see where the new millennium was being celebrated and how. Hour by hour the new millennium passed around the planet. I was never more aware that the earth was really like a giant clock, and that almost everyone was taking part. Local places were all part of the same shared space. An hour after Kiribati, fireworks in New Zealand. No Y2K bug in evidence. It was not the end of the world. Electricity still flowed, water still pumped, ATMs did not fail. The Apocalypse would have to wait a bit longer. And all those people with extra supplies would have to keep them for the next big scare. Two hours later Sydney put on a marvellous show. Fireworks around the harbour, the bridge and opera house backlit by a wild display of pyrotechnics.

The animated image on my TV showed the line moving steadily westwards. Tokyo and Hong Kong now. The celebrations revealed a another global timing. Most Asian countries traditionally use a lunar cycle. Under the Chinese traditional calender, which works on a 60-year cycle, the year 2000 was lunar year 4698. The New Year would traditionally fall on the second new moon after the winter solstice – anytime between 21 January and 19 February. In Korea, Japan and China the millennium celebrations revealed a dual time – traditional and global standard – and the growing importance of the global standard

There was also anxiety, as the fear of the Y2K bug was momentarily in the air. More pervasive was a fear of terrorist outrage, a bombing in a public space to give media attention to an oppressed people, or perhaps to a madman.

Not everywhere celebrated. In Pakistan and Afghanistan the official authorities refused to celebrate what they considered was a foreign festival. Many Muslim fundamentalists consciously sought to distance themselves from this global event. In Dhaka, capital of Bangladesh, 500 police were called in to stop revellers from drinking alcohol. And in Israel rabbis banned New Year celebrations. The silences revealed much about the resistances to globalization.

The line kept moving. A rush of events now. Rome. Berlin. Then there was Paris. It did not disappoint. The Eiffel Tower was so ablaze with fireworks I thought it was going to take off. The French had something to celebrate; not only did their festivities go really well, but the British seemed to have fluffed theirs. The London Eye (a giant ferris-wheel) failed to work, the river of fire on the Thames never materialized, and watching the Queen hold hands with commoners was like watching a distant elderly aunt try to fake jollity at a family event among people she didn't really like.

Quiet across the Atlantic. That was when we needed an Atlantis to take up the slack. But soon there was South America. Who knew that it stuck out so far east, well before New York?

The high-point in time for me, like everyone else I assume, was when the New Year came to my own neighbourhood. Celebrating with friends, drinking champagne and watching the revelry in Times Square. Midnight passed on to the Mid-West, the mountain zone and then the West coast, but my interest was waning. The line continued on to French Polynesia in the South Pacific, one of the last areas on earth to see in the New Year, but by then I was deep in sleep. The local day after the global night before.

The millennium celebrations have a number of lessons for us. The obvious lesson is that they showed us the power and significance of global spectacles. They made us realize the shared yet different experience as people around the world celebrated the same thing at different times. They revealed that global events are concentrated in the big world cities, the places that lit up as midnight passed over them. The rural parts of the same country remained darker, less connected, at least in terms of global imagery. Another lesson: the global spectacle was made possible by a global metric that had been developed more than a century before. The global event had its roots in the nineteenth century.

The millennium celebrations were not the inauguration of globalization, but the high-point of a major phase of it that began in the nineteenth century. And even that was not the first round of globalization. There have been three phases of it. In the first, the Columbian exchange from 1492 to $c.$ 1865, the moving force was economic globalization – what I will term a political internationalization and limited cultural globalization. In the second, from $c.$ 1865 to 1989, economic globalization carried on apace but there was also a political internationalization. The third phase, since 1989, has included economic, political and cultural globalization. It is unique in its wider scope and deeper impact of all three types of globalization, but it is tied to previous phases. The current round is one of reglobalization.

The First Phase of Globalization

1492. The Columbian encounter inaugurated a global world. While empires had extended control outwards from imperial centres to distant peripheries, the world was largely a system of regional empires and separate hemispheric ecologies. Alexander the Great momentarily brought Asia within Europe's compass, and the classical world included North Africa as well as Western Europe. But the world was linked more by distant treaties and long-distance trade than it was by regular interaction. And there was a substantial distinction between the east and west hemispheres, often called the Old and New Worlds.

The New World was populated by people from Asia sometime between 40,000 and 15,000 years ago, at the end of the great cooling of the Pleistocene. A polar ice thaw created a landbridge between Asia and North America. The early immigrants soon dispersed into the continental interior and down into South America. This population movement took place before the domestication of animals in the Old World. Throughout Africa, Asia and Europe humans developed agriculture and kept cattle, horses, pigs and ducks. Measles, smallpox and chicken-pox were just some of the illnesses that originated with domesticated animals. Generations of close contact eventually created a genetic resistance to these diseases. They could be painful and debilitating, but they became less fatal. It was a different story in the New World, where there was much less domestication of animals. Perhaps agriculture was so productive and game so plentiful that there was less pressure to do so. Whatever the combination of factors, the end result was two separate worlds, two hemispheric germ pools.

A major consequence of the encounter between the Old World and the New after 1492 was what has been referred to as a demographic holocaust. The population of the New World was approximately 54 million around 1490. By 1650 that population had fallen to just over 5 million. The cause was the introduction of diseases from the Old World for which the indigenous peoples had no immunity. The result was a tragedy of epic proportions. Almost three out of every four people perished. The Europeans overwhelmed everything they encountered, less because of their technological sophistication, organization or religious ideology, more because of the secret weapons – secret even to them – that were the diseases and germs they carried. This population catastrophe made it easier for the Europeans to gain control. Their ways and religious faith were vindicated by the fact that they survived while the indigenous peoples died in their millions. The Christians' deity did seem to favour the newcomers with the most precious gift – life itself, and the acceptance of Christianity seems less strange in the light of the European survival in the face of indigenous population collapse.

The demographic holocaust was just one consequence of the Columbian encounter. Others followed. The decline in the local populations necessitated imported labour to work in the mines and on the estates. The slave trade shipped close to 10 million people from Africa to the New World. Then there was the biotic exchange. New World crops such as corn (i.e., maize) and potatoes enriched the diets of the whole world, leading to population increases in Europe. The Irish peasantry, for example, rapidly adopted the potato as a staple crop. Tomatoes, sunflowers, peanuts and turkeys moved east, while horses, hens, cattle, pigs, sugar-cane and wheat moved west. Major environmental changes were wrought as a variety of plants and animals were dispersed around the world. When we pick tomatoes in Europe or ride horses in America, we are taking part in a process of globalization that began when Columbus landed in the New World. The encounter bridged the hemispheric divide in a series of transactions and exchanges of people, plants, animals and viruses that created a global world.

To be sure, there is no straight line from 1492 to the present day. It is more accurate to consider a series of re-globalizations as different parts of Europe and the New World were bound together in a various ways. Take the case of the fur trade in North America. In the early seventeenth century, the Dutch, English and French competed to dominate a trade in which Native Americans played a key role. Their local hunting knowledge was used to find and kill the beavers that ended up as hats on the heads of the wealthy in the cities of Paris, Amsterdam and London. The fur trade involved the commodification of nature and the restructuring of Native American society. What had been hunted for use value now was sought for exchange value. Beaver pelts paid for guns, knives, blankets, kettles and alcohol. The rituals that limited hunting were replaced by the dictates of an insatiable market. Beavers were overhunted. The plentiful supplies in the Hudson Valley in the early seventeenth century were soon depleted. Local tribes lost their economic power while groups such as the Iroquois, situated further north and west, began to play a pivotal role, straddling the line between the European merchants and the ready supplies available further west. Native Americans fought among themselves as well as against the Europeans to ensure a continued supply of beaver pelts. The nexus of the fur trade changed the ecology, trade patterns, the material life and the geopolitics of Native American life in the north-east and even much further west. And Native Americans were not simply passive victims in the process. The Iroquois' empire was based on their ability to control the supply and exchange of pelts for a European market.

Globalization was the process whereby local places were incorporated into the space of a global economy and the global economy was articulated through a series of connected places. On the banks of the Hudson, at present-day Albany, the trade in the seventeenth century – furs for alcohol and iron tools – was more than just an exchange of goods, it was the transformation of place into space. Local ways and practices were transformed by the new connections to distant markets and foreign influences. Local ways were transformed by global market forces.

We can see an emerging global economy by the end of the eighteenth century. The colonies of European powers could be self-sufficient as well as tied to wider trade flows. In South America, the Spaniar trated in small numbers, ruled over large peasant m self-sufficient rural economy. But the mined gold and silver flc Spain,[2] while rich colonists were able to buy goods manufactured in Europe. In the Caribbean and along the coasts of Brazil and the Carolinas, tropical goods – sugar, coffee, rice, cotton – were planted and harvested by slave labour and shipped to Europe. The sugar islands were agricultural gold-mines, eagerly sought. In 1763, during negotiations over the treaty that ended the Seven Years War, the French decided they were willing to give up Canada in order to keep the two islands of Guadeloupe and Martinique. Many in Britain felt that the French had hoodwinked the British negotiators. What could you do with vast frozen lands, whereas everyone knew how valuable sugar islands were?

In North America, two systems were in operation. In the South, slave plantations produced rice and sugar. In other parts of the South and most of the Northern areas, small farmers produced grain, butter and meat that was sold in the West Indies. The money was used to buy goods manufactured in Europe. In 1700 most of Britain's trade was with its European neighbours. By 1750 North America accounted for one-third of Britain's export trade. A quarter of all France's commercial operations on the eve of the French Revolution was the sugar trade with the two sugar islands. On the eve of the American Revolution, a global economy was in place.

The integrated nature of the networks is apparent when we consider the first phase of the Industrial Revolution in Britain. By 1775 two-thirds of the value of its trade involved either a source or destination overseas. Between 1780 and 1840 cotton manufacture in Britain was the leading sector in the new forms of manufacturing. Over half of all Britain's exports for most of this phase were cotton goods. The raw material came from plantations in the Caribbean and North America, while three-quarters of the cotton goods were exported to Africa, America and Asia. In 1850 India was taking one-quarter of all British cotton exports. The global network allowed cheap imports and guaranteed exports. It was Britain's global connections that created the Industrial Revolution.

At this time, we can barely identify political globalization, if we mean by that term some form of move to world government. However, there was a growing internationalization of the state. In Europe it was apparent that national wealth and security was dependent on overseas possessions. In the wake of the Columbian encounter, European powers scrambled to gain a piece of the action. The wealth of Spain, its bullion fleets crammed with gold and silver sailing to Cadiz, prompted more than one European country to venture overseas. The Swedes landed in what is now Delaware (the major city of that small state is Wilmington, named for a Swedish queen). The Dutch formed both East India and West India Companies to take advantage of trading opportunities in Asia and America. The French and English competed for spice and sugar islands around the world and for territorial control in Asia, Africa and America.

Global geopolitics was dominated by an economic nationalism that held the mercantilistic belief that if it was the business of the state to promote economic endeavours, the best way to do this was to stimulate foreign trade. Initially, the accumulation of gold and silver was considered paramount; the emphasis then switched to the belief that wealth lay in the import of cheap raw materials and the export of expensive manufactured goods. Mercantilism held that the world's wealth was limited and, like a giant cake, could only be obtained at the expense of others. It became imperative to grab as big a slice as possible.

The state was internationalized. Its mission was to increase foreign trade, control foreign holdings and encourage colonization. Overseas territorial annexation laid the basis for economic growth and national development. The nation–state was called on to make international moves. The overseas expansion of European powers in the seventeenth and eighteenth centuries signalled the internationalism of those states. The distinction between global and national was no longer clear. When national interests were connected to global repositioning, the state was an international actor.

Global politics was dominated by struggles for world supremacy. In the sixteenth century Spain and Portugal held the stage with their vast and rich holdings in America and Asia. By the end of the sixteenth century, Spain had carved out a huge overseas empire in the Americas and amassed a considerable fortune, which allowed the Spanish Crown to pursue its role as defender of the Catholic faith in Europe. The very success of its imperial position was to provide the basis of its subsequent decline. Spain illustrates an early example of what historian Paul Kennedy has described as imperial overstretch.[3] Superpowers arise on the basis of their military and economic strength. Challenges, however, are made to their dominance, and, to maintain their position, more of the resources are devoted to shoring up their geopolitical position and defending their insecure frontiers. Imperial responsibilities undercut the economic strength of the state. Spain was committed to ensuring its continued dominance in the Americas, safeguarding its commercial trade and fighting numerous wars in Europe, especially against the Protestant English and the Moslem Turks. Imperial overstretch was heightened by the massive increase in the costs of war, the failure of the Spanish government to raise sufficient taxes, and the existence for Spain of 'too many enemies to fight, too many frontiers to defend'.[4] The strain of overstretch was exacerbated in Spain by the increasing disdain for commercial enterprises, rapid inflation, the loss of imperial markets and the eventual collapse of indigenous industries. The defeat of the Armada in 1588 marked the beginning of the end of military, economic and political confidence. There were recurring fiscal crises caused by increases in royal expenditure just as the income from Spain's American mines began to run dry. The national debt was summarily cancelled in 1596 and again in 1607, with a consequent huge decline in public confidence. By 1600 interest payments totalled two-thirds of all state revenues, and, by the 1650s, Spain was no longer a superpower.

In the early seventeenth century global power began to shift north from Spain towards France, England, and the Dutch United Provinces. The Dutch, in particular, made inroads in Asia, America and Africa. Batavia, New Amsterdam (later renamed New York) and Cape Town were the beads on a long thread of world trade. But, by the end of the century, not only Spain and Portugal but the Dutch too were losing their grip on world power. The main players were now Britain and France, and their struggle for mastery encompassed the world. Wars between the two countries were fought in Europe, India, Africa and America. France's defeat in one of them, the Seven Years War (1756–63), marked the beginnings of British pre-eminence on the world stage.

There was a globalization of politics, but not a political globalization. Certain nation–states had been internationalized, but there was not an international agency. National rivalries arose from global repositioning, but global politics did not create a global polity.

Cultural globalization came in a number of forms. The most obvious were the vast migrations of people that redistributed European and African cultures throughout America and parts of Asia. Almost 10 million Africans were transported to the New World, Spaniards and Portuguese went to South and Central America, while French and English colonists landed in North America. These peoples took with them their languages, religions, tastes and habits, beliefs and practices. Spanish became the language of Latin America, French and English were spoken in the North. Roman Catholicism became the dominant religion in Central and Latin America. But, in the process, there was an indigenization as local people crafted the new beliefs onto old deities and traditional ways.

We can draw a distinction between America and Asia. The demographic holocaust in America created more of a blank page for European inscription. In Asia, in contrast, there was no population collapse. Older cultures survived intact; Buddhism, Hinduism and Confucianism were not displaced by Christianity, and local languages persisted. Cultural globalization was most pronounced in the New World.

The flows went into as well as out of Europe. Tobacco smoking, beaver hats, coffee-houses, a love of porcelain, tea and oriental rugs were all consumption patterns connected to a global economy. The rest of the world also became creative sources for the European imagination. The South Seas, for example, was a source of romantic imagery and arcadian longings.

By *c.* 1800 most of the world was brought into European knowing. The last 'unknown' area was the South Pacific. Captain Cook's voyages and the subsequent arrival of British convict ships in Australia in 1788 marked the beginning of formal claims. The mapping of the South Pacific was soon completed. By 1810 all the world was captured within the European cartographic imagination and the intellectual circumnavigation of the globe was complete.

Globalization in this first phase was the enforced incorporation of the world into European control. The story is one of increasing territorial annexation, a widening of the flows of the globalization, and a deepening as the economies and fortunes of Europe and the rest of the world became more intimately linked. A major theme is the competition between European powers for global supremacy. But there was also resistance. European control was rarely welcomed and seldom unchallenged. Resistance took many forms. The American Declaration of Independence in 1776 was opposition to overseas control by the descendants of European colonists. A hard-core economic nationalism was framed by a softer shell of political philosophy to create a justification for imperial break-up and national self-determination. The loss of its American colonies in 1783 (though it kept Canada) did not hinder Britain's economic growth, but it did signal the beginning of a shift in global geopolitics, a move from subjects to citizens and the articulation of a political philosophy that was later to dominate the world. The new USA would undertake its own imperial conquest of the continental interior and, within 200 years, become the world's superpower. But that was in the future.

Throwing off the colonial yoke was not limited to North America. Between 1806 and 1826 there were rumblings in Latin America. The Napoleonic conquest of Spain and Portugal had meant a break with the imperial centre. This allowed the space for the articulation of demands for political freedoms and economic self-determination. The colonial powers differed in their response. The Portuguese allowed an easy transfer into Brazilian independence, but the Spanish resisted. The successful military campaigns of Bolívar, Sucre, San Martin and Bernardo O'Higgins led to independence for a number of countries: Argentina in 1810, Peru in 1821, and Ecuador in 1830. Political independence did not mean economic independence. It meant a transfer of formal political power from a Spanish crown to local elites. National economies were still closely tied to Europe as markets for primary products and as sources of capital and manufactured goods.

The Second Phase of Globalization

The second phase of globalization was *c.* 1865 to 1989. Let me repeat that all my dates are to some degree arbitrary, giving the illusion of distinct beginnings and ends when, in truth, history is like life, which is, as someone once remarked, just one damned thing after another. Historical trends flow through time in loose and messy ways. There are few sharp breaks or divisions. Dates are more symbolic than explanatory. The year 1865 is significant in that it marks the the end of the American Civil War. The cessation of that internal struggle meant that the character of the US was now to be shaped by Northern industry rather than by Southern agrarianism. Westward expansion became the historical motif of the nation, but although the continental aspirations of Manifest Destiny were now given full force, the US also began to make its presence felt on the international stage, along with Germany and other new arrivals, which marks a phase of growing political internationalism.

This second phase of globalization is marked by continuing economic globalization, growing political internationalization and limited cultural globalization. It was not a continuous process. The period 1914–45 constitutes a rupture of world wars and economic depression. Many of the reglobalization trends after this period can be seen as a response to turmoil and economic disintegration.

Economic globalization from *c.* 1865 to 1914 becomes more pronounced. It is a time of low tariffs, an international labour market and relatively free capital mobility. The adoption of the Gold Standard was the nearest thing yet to a universal form of exchange, and it encouraged capital mobility. This regime of free trade did not reign everywhere; critics of the time called it British internationalism. British overseas investments were twice those of France and five times those of the US. It was an economic globalization firmly centred in London, the pivot of the international trading system, the sun of the trading universe. Other countries, for example, France, Germany and the US, were also involved, albeit in their smaller trading empires. More areas of the world were being drawn into global economic transactions. The global system was neither fair nor equitable. It was a system dominated by merchants, manufacturers and investors, one in which the rich countries sought out raw materials, markets and investment opportunities.

Economic integration was reinforced by changes in transportation that compressed space and time. Railways had been introduced before 1865 but were limited to partial networks in a handful of countries. After 1865 there was a widening and deepening of the railway network around the world. In 1870 there were only 125,000 miles of track; by 1911 this had increased to 657,000 miles. The railways brought places closer together in terms of the time it took to get people or goods from A to B. This space–time shrinkage compressed the world. Far away from the tracks, life may not have been unchanged, but the whistle of the train speeded up the world.

There was also an expansion in shipping. In 1865 most of the world's shipping trade was carried by sailing ships. By 1914 the more reliable steam engine had replaced the vagaries of the wind. Steamers carried emigrants across the Atlantic, transported beef from Latin America, tea from China and iron railway lines to India. The Suez Canal (1869) and Panama Canal (1914) cut world shipping times even further.

The formation of a global economy involved the incorporation of additional areas of the world. Large parts of Africa, Asia and even faraway islands in the South Pacific were annexed to a global economic order. Overseas territories provided cheap raw materials, secured markets for manufactured goods, were sources of national prestige and used as pawns in the great game of global geopolitics.

This period was also an age of imperialism involving the territorial annexation of land and peoples into colonies of European powers and the US. A neo-mercantilist doctrine emerged that argued for the protection of home industries and for the possession of overseas colonies that would ensure access to cheap raw materials and a captive market, both of which could be denied to competitors. National pride and prestige came into play as more of the world was swallowed up and countries sought to claim a piece of the action and avoid global exclusion. The German Historical School promoted protection of German industry and possession of overseas colonies. Under Bismarck, Germany, which had been laggard in the industrial revolution, soon surpassed Britain in steel production and embarked on an imperial drive for colonies.

Africa provides a classic example. When Britain announced unilateral control of Egypt in 1882 and Germany claimed territory throughout Africa, the stage was set for large-scale partition. A conference was called by Bismarck that met in Berlin in 1884, at which claims and counter-claims were put forward. The conference did little to solve the issues, but by drawing up rules for successful claims, it declared an open season. In 1880

European power in Africa was restricted to coastal areas. By the eve of the First World War, the whole of Africa, apart from Liberia and Ethiopia, was partitioned into European colonies.

It was not only European powers that were involved. The US played a significant role. After the Civil War there was substantial agreement among the political and economic elites in the country that overseas expansion was necessary to provide safe investment sites and markets for manufactured goods. Overseas expansion would allow steady and sustained growth of a kind that would counter economic depression at home and forestall social unrest. This expansionist urge was built into the very fabric of the nation through its westward growth, its Manifest Destiny, and the continual invoking of the frontier as a call to arms, a legacy that persists today as 'Space – the final frontier'. There was a counter-current, a more populist expression of the need to concentrate on domestic matters and concerns. This expansionist/isolationist polarity was to cause tension in the US's role in world affairs. This tension persists in a variety of forms, from the US's ambiguous relationship with the UN, to domestic popular opinion that has continually to be persuaded of the need for foreign 'interventions'.

In Asia the US was obsessed by China. A series of island annexations – Midway (1867), Hawaii (1888), Guam (1898), the Philippines (1898) and Wake Island (1899) – were stepping-stones to Asia. There was also US expansionism in the Caribbean after Spain's defeat in the Spanish–American war. Puerto Rico was annexed in 1898, Cuba became part of the semi-formal empire, and punitive expeditions were sent to various countries to impose US commercial interests: Panama (1903), Nicaragua (1909–33) and the Dominican Republic (1916–24). Under the Monroe Doctrine, first enunciated in 1823 but only effectively imposed at the end of the century, Latin America became the US's backyard. European powers were neither welcome nor encouraged, and the US imagined itself as arbiter of the political economy of the region.

One of the social commentators of the time, J. A. Hobson, argued that imperialism was an artificial stimulation of nationalism.[5] The tap-root of imperialism, as he called it, was the influence of investors eager to take over foreign areas in order to secure new areas for profitable investment. He believed that the state was being over-influenced by rich investors to undertake costly imperial adventures with grave political risks. His response was to call for a more even distribution of wealth and a genuine democratization of the state. It was, and remains, a noble vision. Overseas expansions and foreign interventions deflect attention from domestic reform and social emancipation at home. The counter-argument was summed up in a remark attributed to Cecil Rhodes: 'If you wish to avoid civil war then you must become an imperialist.'

Britain not only had its formal empire, which was territory under direct political control, but also an informal empire consisting of those territories and countries that were economically, but not politically, tied to Britain. Imperialism was a sign of failure for the colonizing powers. Formal empires were expensive to run and colonial powers ran the risk of military embarrassment. Foreign fields could become quagmires that sucked in troops and money, deflated international prestige and squandered domestic political capital. For Britain the real success story was the informal empire in Latin America. Britain had huge interests in Latin America, including shipping and railways, banks and insurance companies, the control of the Peruvian guano and Chilean nitrate industries, and ownership of the utility companies that provided transportation and water in the region's cities. Investments in trade, commodities, shipping and public utilities provided returns two per cent higher than British colonial government securities. By 1913 Britain had capital investments of almost a billion pounds sterling in Latin America – a quarter of all British foreign capital investment.

Imperialism signified a failure to successfully incorporate an economy into the metropolitan centre without direct annexation. This could happen if local elites resisted their incorporation. The history of the British in India is one of authority imposed in the face of non-colloborative local elites. The transition from informal to formal empire occurred as the collaborative elite system broke down. After all, you only need to intervene in a banana republic when the bananas fail to arrive. The local elites in Latin America, in contrast, welcomed British investment. It was Latin America's elites who organized the state and held the local resistance in check. Collaborative elites facilitated European economic penetration.

Annexation could also occur to forestall the actions of other would-be colonial powers. Some of Britain's colonial involvement in Africa and the Middle East was, in part, due to the need to protect trading routes to India from the designs of other European powers. The costs of formal imperialism were accepted so that Britain's geopolitical dominance could be maintained. The partition of Africa into separate European spheres of influence was a scramble for territory that was exacerbated when some European countries panicked about being left out of the race. Even tiny Belgium felt that national pride dictated an African presence. Hence the Belgian Congo, the setting for Conrad's great novel *Heart of Darkness* (1902), the basis for Coppola's Vietnam movie, *Apocalypse Now*.

There was resistance to imperialism. Let us consider just three. The Boxer Rebellion of 1898 marked a nationalist response in China. At the time, China was a failing empire that had been losing out to foreign powers eager to capture its markets. By the beginning of the nineteenth century Britain had control of the opium trade. Opium was grown in Bengal and shipped to China. Official Chinese resistance to the trade (it created social problems at home as well as a negative balance of payments) led to the Opium Wars of 1839–1842. Britain won and imposed a commercial order. In the 1842 Treaty of Nanking, Hong Kong was ceded to Britain. China was humiliated by the defeats. Other colonial powers were also seeking access to Chinese markets. In the 1895 Treaty of Shomonoseki, Taiwan was given to Japan. There was a fear that China was being swallowed by foreign powers. At the same time floods and other natural disasters caused unrest.

The Boxers, a group devoted to martial arts (their full name was the Righteous and Harmonious Fists), were an anti-foreign movement that became allied with the Qing dynasty seeking to throw out the interlopers. Particular resentment was focused on the Christian missionaries, who were undertaking programmes of conversion. The Boxers led an uprising in 1898. The siege of the foreign legations in Beijing ended with the arrival of an international force of 20,000 troops; resistance was eventually crushed and the Dowager Empress was forced to flee.

The empire of the Zulu, a Bantu-speaking people in southern Africa, was at its peak in the early nineteenth century. A well-disciplined army, notably under Shaka, had imposed a territorial coherence and political unity. From *c.* 1840 to 1870 parts of Zululand were ceded to Boers (whites of Dutch descent) and the British. Zulu resistance began in 1870 when the new king, Cetshwayo, vowed to restore Zulu dominance. The British responded by sending in a punitive force of almost 10,000 in 1879. After intense fighting, including the famous defence of Rorke's Drift, the Zulu were defeated, Cetshwayo was exiled, territory was confiscated and tribal reserves were established. The British government annexed Zululand in 1887. Simmering resistance led to further uprisings in 1888 and 1906. These were crushed and Zululand was divided into native reserves, Crown property and tracts that were passed to white farmers.

The Philippines became known to the Europeans in 1521 when Ferdinand Magellan first landed there. By 1600 it was under Spanish dominance. There was ongoing resistance, especially from the Muslim population. Filipino nationalism was slow to develop among the myriad peoples in the many islands. But by the nineteenth century an independence movement was emerging. In 1891 José Rizal y Mercado (a Chinese mestizo) established Liga Filipina. He was arrested by the Spanish and executed in 1896. In the same year, Tagalong speakers numbering almost a quarter of a million took part in an insurrection against Spanish power. A republic was declared in June 1898. However, Spain ceded the Philippines to the US in December 1898 and the following month US troops arrived there. Insurrection took the form of a guerilla campaign. Vietnam was not the first war the US was to fight against a nationalist movement in Asia. The US ran the country through a series of governor-generals, but Filipino resistance continued, albeit moving from armed struggle to political negotiations. It was only in 1946 that the Philippines became a sovereign independent state.

Prior to 1914 anti-colonial feeling was prevalent around the world, but it consisted of anti-colonial outbursts rather than successful campaigns for independence. There was very little success. The Boxers were defeated, the Zulu lost their land, and, in the Philippines, the Americans replaced the Spanish as colonial masters. A similar tale could be told of many places. Successful political de-colonization would have to wait many more years.

From 1865 to 1914 there was a growing economic integration. It tended to be enforced and unfair, for this was an economic globalization imposed by European powers and the US. But rather than a single world economy, it was a series of local globalizations that occurred as colonial powers sought to create their own world networks. The one exception was Britain, whose economic success and dominance was both reflected and embodied in its truly global trading system.

There was cultural fall-out from this economic integration. Take sports. One reason that soccer is the world game is because of Britain's dominance in the nineteenth century. The British took their language and games with them as well as their armies, clerks and traders. Soccer is particularly strong in South America, never part of Britain's formal empire (Guyana excepted), but a major part of its trading empire. Through much of Central America and the Caribbean, in contrast, part of the US's semi-formal empire, baseball dominates. Language, sports, manners and customs circulated the world, sometimes taking root, sometimes not. Cricket for example, became important only in the formal empire: South Africa, Australia, New Zealand, India, Sri Lanka and Pakistan, though not in Canada. Rugby has a similar pattern, although Argentina has a shared allegiance to both soccer and rugby. The Fiji Islands, affected more by Welsh missionaries, also has a greater emphasis on rugby rather than soccer. Accident and chance played a role in the precise form of cultural diffusion, but there was a similar dynamic; customs and language were diffused around the world. This is not the same thing as cultural globalization, the move towards a global culture. But it was a case of growing hybridity and de-territorialization as the English language was spoken outside of the Anglo world, and soccer and cricket were played beyond the green fields of the home country.

There was also an empire of signs. The experiences of the colonized were given shape, form and meaning by the metropolitan centre. The production of knowledge was like other manufacturing processes: raw materials were shipped in from the periphery for value-added work; then shipped back around the world. Global power and politics played an important role in the production of ideas. We are aware that knowledge production is dependant on time. The forward march of knowledge is a familiar figure of speech that draws on this temporal dimension. But knowledge is also produced in place as well as time. The place of knowledge production can be as important as the time of production. The geopolitical terms used to describe the world are a good example. When we use the term Middle East or South-East Asia, for example, we are describing the world from a specific location, a world that was originally centred on London. We take these terms so much for granted that we often forget they are a convention related to Britain's imperial position. If a great empire had been centred in Jerusalem, then Britain would now be the Middle West, the US would be the Far West and Chile would be in South-West America. A later US dominance was imposed when the term *West* was used to describe the bipolarity of the world irrespective of hemispheric location. Despite its oft-used description as *West*, Europe is still in the eastern hemisphere.

It was not only in geographical descriptions that the bias was apparent. The metropolitan centres created knowledge systems from the bias of a particular place. Anthropology, sociology, history and the social sciences and humanities were produced in the context of an imperial system of power. Indeed, the knowledge reproduced this system. Comparative knowledge systems such as anthropology and sociology created a hierarchy of stages that most often peaked at the imperial centre. The stages of humankind, comparative religions, the evolution of society, levels of civilization were all devices used to grade and sift the world into hierarchical classifications. Theory production was part of the imperial project: classify and conquer. It was not just an economic system, but an empire of signs, a global knowledge system that turned local signification into a world-wide understanding, all from a specific location. There was a physical legacy. Kew Gardens, the British Museum, the great libraries and scientific organizations were all part of a global system of knowledge accumulation, classification and production. The material culture, meaning and significance of the periphery was annexed as well as its raw materials and commodities. There was an intellectual as well as economic appropriation.

But there were alternative readings, even in the centre. Let me describe one fracture in my own intellectual discipline. Geography grew as an academic subject in the late nineteenth century. There had been cosmographers and geographers well before this, but geography as an organized intellectual discipline really makes its appearance with the growth of imperialism. The title of the 'Society for Commercial Geography and Promotion of German Interests Abroad', founded in Germany in 1878, encapsulates the general mood. Geographers became involved in imperial debates. Francis Younghusband's *India and Pakistan* (1910) justified the British invasion of Tibet. One of the best-known British geographers was Halford Mackinder (1861–1947). In his writings he gave intellectual substance to patriotism and British commercial interests. Born into the middle class, he became a member of the establishment committed to the British state and the existing order. He was a director of the London School of Economics from 1903 to 1908 and a Member of Parliament from 1902 to 1922. His most famous paper was read to the Royal Geographical Society as 'The Geographical Pivot of History'. Mackinder outlined a theory of geopolitics that argued for a containment of Russia and a strategic rationale for British overseas presence, a presence sanctified by the need to save world civilization. Britain's empire was justified as a containment of barbarism and a support for civilization. His arguments were developed further in *Democratic Ideals and Reality* (1904). For Mackinder, geography was an aid to statecraft.

Peter Kropotkin (1842–1921) occupies roughly the same time and intellectual space as Mackinder. But although he was a Russian aristocrat, he became a fervent critic of the existing order. He was secretary of the Imperial Russian Geographical Society and undertook fieldwork in Asiatic Russia. A critic of the Czarist system, he was forced to leave the country in 1876. He landed in England and devoted his time to developing ideas of mutual cooperation.

Two geographers, but with very different approaches. They stand at opposite ends of a continuum of engagement. One was a servant of the ruling class, committed to Britain's imperial venture. The other was a radical who proposed the ideas of 'No Government, the rights of the individual, of local action and free agreement'. While one supported the state, the other spoke out against 'State almightiness, centralization and discipline'. While one saw geographic education as essential if 'educated classes were not to loose their grip and their influence over the half-educated proletariat', the other saw that it was the task of geography

> to interest the child in the great phenomena of nature, to awaken the desire of knowing and explaining. Geography must render, moreover, another far more important service, it must teach us ... that we are all brethren, whatever our nationality.... It must show that each nationality brings its own precious building stone for the general development of the commonwealth, and that only

small parts of each nation are interested in maintaining national hatreds and jealousies.

One imperial centre, two very different voices. One forwarding a national geopolitics, the other an early proponent of a mutual international cooperation. Political geography lost its way when it followed Mackinder rather than Kropotkin. Kropotkin never used the term globalization, but he was writing about its positive forces when faced with a dangerous nationalism.

The period from *c.* 1865 to 1914 was marked by an internationalization of politics. There were countless international meetings, conferences and conventions, for example the meridian conferences mentioned at the outset of this chapter, which laid down transnational standards and arrangements. But it was not only the political elites who were looking for international cooperation. The International Workingmen's Association was formed in 1864 to give substance to international solidarity. And in sports we see the beginning of international competitions. FIFA, the Federation of International Football Associations, was formed in Zurich in 1904, while the first Olympic Games of the modern era took place in 1896 in Athens. The moving force was Baron Pierre de Coubertin, who believed that reviving the ancient games would counter the worst excesses of nationalism.

We tend to think of global communications as a function of our time. But the earlier era laid down many of the institutional arrangements that we still use today. Postal services, for example, had been organized by state. There was no international standard that allowed the easy movement of mail between countries. A conference was held in Paris in 1863 to achieve standardization. At the Congress of Bern in 1874, 22 countries signed the International Postal Convention. The signatories were all European countries, plus Egypt and the US. By 1878 the list had expanded and the name was changed to the Universal Postal Union, and today almost all countries are members. Signatories adhere to an important principle: the territory of all member countries is a single space. A letter posted in one country to another is paid for in the originating country but delivered without charge by the postal service of the country of destination, just as if it were domestic mail. It was, and is, an amazing example of the globalization of communication that aided international communication and interaction. The First and Second International, FIFA, the Olympic Games and the Postal Union are just some of the many international organizations that were established in the second wave of globalization.

There was a tension. The internationalization of politics not only reduced national frictions, it could exaggerate them. Just as the Olympics nationalizes sporting events – individuals compete for their country, medals ceremonies include national flags and anthems, medals tables gauge national rankings – so with other organizations. The conferences and organizations meant to transcend national differences could sometimes reinforce them.

The second wave of globalization suffered a major disjuncture. The 'Thirty Years War' from 1914 to 1945 is marked by two world wars and a global economic depression. But the horror of one world war after another led many countries to seek the basis for a renewed integration. The charter of the UN was first drawn up in 1945 to provide a forum for international dialogue. Regional alliances were also formed. The Council of Europe in 1949 was followed by the European Coal and Steel Community in 1952, the European Economic Community in 1958 and the European Community in 1967. From the ashes of the Second World War there has been a conscious attempt to create a unified Europe.

The economic depression of the 1930s arose from a narrow economic nationalism. In the new post-war world, rules and organizations were established to halt the world economy from slipping into the downward spiral caused by national economic protectionism. In 1944, at Bretton Woods in New England, a new economic order was created that stressed free trade. The World Bank and International Monetary Fund (IMF) were created. Fixed exchange rates were established to give stability to international trade. The UN, IMF and World Bank were systems of international regulation that provided the backbone of a more integrated world. It was a world now more centred on the US. While the UN is headquartered in New York, the IMF and the World Bank are only a few blocks from the White House in Washington, DC.

Reglobalizations

The broad picture I have presented is of two major waves of globalization in which the world was brought closer together. The third wave, which begins in earnest after 1989, is marked by an increasing economic, political and cultural globalization. These trends will be explored in subsequent chapters.

The waves of globalization have left a legacy. Just as waves sweeping onto a shore affect the topography of the beach, which, in turn, shapes the flow of subsequent waves, so the waves of globalization have impacted on places, and the character of places has in turn affected the subsequent flows of global contact. We can imagine the world as a series of places in a continual process of reglobalization. I will expand this point with reference to a case study – Sydney in Australia. Sydney grew as an outpost of the British empire, developed as a primate city, and, more recently, blossomed into a global city. An understanding of Sydney's growth and change allows us to see how pulses of globalization affect one city over time.

Sydney first became global in 1788 when it was established as an antipodean gulag for the British state. The newly discovered country was initially a solution to Britain's overcrowded gaols. Before 1776, generations of convicts had been shipped to Virginia and neighbouring colonies, but the War of Independence ended this arrangement. Sydney's first permanent European settlers were convicts and gaolers sent to the other side of the world. During the course of the nineteenth century this initially carceral city broadened its functions. Sydney was an economic node in the British imperial system, a colonial entrepôt city, the transmission point between the wider world and Australia's interior, which was being commodified to provide wheat, timber, minerals. These goods were sent to Britain, which, in turn, shipped back labour, capital and finished materials. Sydney was an important point in these economic transactions, and the political and economic capital of New South Wales.

Prior to 1901 Australia was, in reality, a collection of semi-autonomous states, including New South Wales, South Australia, Victoria, Queensland and West Australia. Each state acted as a separate economic and political unit with its own capital city, respectively Sydney, Adelaide, Melbourne, Brisbane and Perth. Though Sydney dominated the state of New South Wales, it was not the only gateway city in Australia. The other cities played similar roles for their respective states. Indeed, throughout the second half of the nineteenth century, Melbourne could lay legitimate claim to be Australia's dominant city. After the Gold Rush of the 1850s in Victoria, the growth of 'Marvellous Melbourne' was spectacular. And when the new federal state needed a temporary capital before Canberra was laid out and landscaped, Melbourne was selected. In the period when Australia's globalization hinged on primary commodity production, Melbourne dominated. It housed the economic elite and the headquarters of the commodity companies. Melbourne's claim to being Australia's global city was reinforced when it hosted the 1956 Olympic Games; 3,000 athletes arrived there from 67 countries.

In the second half of the twentieth century the competition to be Australia's gateway city was fought between Sydney and Melbourne. Each city represented the hopes and aspirations of their respective state governments as well as private sector interests. But in comparison to the US, state governments played an enormous role in the growth machine and civic boosterism. Both groups realized that Australia could only sustain one global city. They both wanted it to be their city.

Sydney began to pull away from Melbourne in terms of international recognition. While both of them were approximately the same size (including the outer suburban areas; the figure is now approximately 4 million for Sydney and 3.5 million for Melbourne), Sydney began to achieve more international visibility. The completion of the Opera House in 1973 gave the city a globally recognized icon. The project was begun in 1955 when the Danish architect Joern Utzon submitted the winning design entry. When it opened, the Opera House joined the Harbour Bridge in giving the city international recognition with a global signifier. For example, to celebrate the worldwide millennium 2000 celebrations, CNN's news cameras covered the Sydney celebrations. No other Australian city was as visible to an international audience.

An economic shift also occurred when Britain joined the European Community in 1973. As part of the entry requirements, Britain had to jettison its long-established trading relations with Australia and New Zealand. Australia now had to operate in a global market rather than an imperial one. This initiated a new round of globalization. In the course of it, economic orientation shifted to the Pacific Rim; 60 per cent of Australia's exports now go to Japan. There was also a reconnection with the world's financial system as the links with London were adjusted. It is in this recent reglobalization that Sydney has emerged as Australia's global city. In the past twenty years it has become the major destination for foreign investment and the leading choice for the headquarters of foreign banks, multinational corporations and high-tech companies. As Australia has reglobalized to an interconnected economy, Sydney has become its global gateway city.

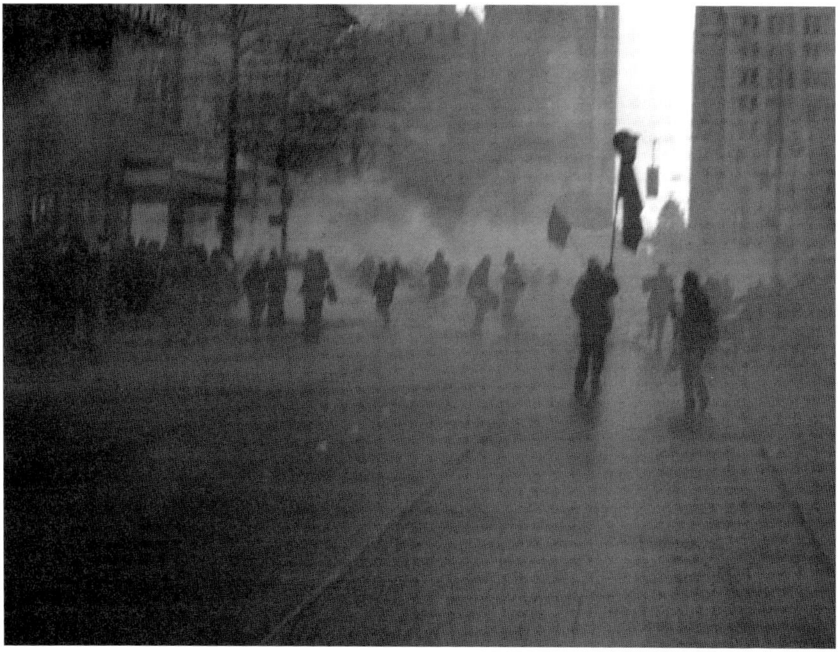

CHAPTER THREE

Does a Global Polity Mean the End of the Nation–State?

In September 2000, 149 leaders of countries from all around the world met at the UN in New York City for a three-day meeting, billed as the Millennium Summit. It was a big event, one of the largest-ever single gatherings of heads of state. Another event in the same month of the same year was the IMF's meeting held in Prague. Not only were members of the IMF in the beautiful Baroque city, there were also demonstrators, many of them bearing slogans that read *No to Globalization*. Both events can be seen as examples of political globalization. Political globalization can be defined in a number of ways: as a move towards global government; a trend towards more global governance; the creation of a global citizenry. I will examine each of these in this chapter.

The image of a world government has long been both a dream and a nightmare. There are the 'one-worlders', who see the problems of the world primarily as the result of the division of the world into separate and competing nation–states. If only we could all come together, then many of the world's problems would disappear. There are few who are so dewy-eyed, but there is a firm belief, held by some, that only global government can provide us with a solid foundation for lasting peace and prosperity. At the millennium summit Václav Havel, President of the Czech Republic, and someone who knows personally about the repressive power of the state, suggested that the 'UN should transform from a large community of governments, diplomats and officials into a joint institution for each inhabitant of the planet . . . and guarantee global legislation'. The one-worlders have a point. The twentieth century showed the spiral of destruction that nationalism can create. Rogue states, competing states, states against their own peoples have all been the context for frightful dramas of human suffering. If we could temper the power of states then we could lessen the chances for repeating such hideous affairs. On the other side, there are many, including the anarchists marching in Prague and nationalists around the world, who see world government as the imposition of a single, invariably sinister, organization whose draconian powers would sweep away local uniqueness and national distinctiveness. Globalization is often discussed in populist rhetoric as an acid that would eat away at locality and national sovereignty. There is a point here. Global government, if it came to pass, would create a single enormous power centre. And with what end? If you have a worry about state power, what about global power? If the nation–state is a scary power centre, how about a global government? What recourse would you have as an individual or small group against a global government? The rich and powerful have a way of controlling things; that's what makes them rich and powerful. Give them world government and there is no telling what they might do.

The one-worlders posit a benign globality that can save us from the worst excesses of nationalism and other dangerous doctrines of othering; the anarchists and nationalists point to a sinister globality, a concentration of power and influence impervious to local and national concerns.

How far are we moving towards global government? There are those who see an inexorable slide towards a global superstate. A simplistic reading suggests that globalization, in its various forms, is leading to global government as the nation–states decline. My take on the evidence available is that globalization may be leading to a global polity and governance, but not necessarily to global government; in addition, the nation–state is enduring, and, in some cases, is being strengthened by the very forces of globalization. When those leaders were meeting in New York, they were representing different countries in a single forum. They were not giving up national sovereignty, but simply using it to benefit from, and control, the flows and forces of globalization. Globalization is *not* undermining the nation–state, it is reshaping it, and globalization, in turn, is being channelled and shaped by nation–states.

There has been a shift towards a more global governance that is less concerned with government as we commonly know it, and more concerned with regulation and control. In the post-1944 era, and particularly since 1989, there has been increased global regulation of world trade and finance. Although the picture of floating exchange rates and rapid capital inflows and outflows would seem to suggest an unregulated market, in fact the global economy has been governed by a series of institutions and rules. In effect, there has been more global regulation that has not been subject to democratic accountability. Many of those who fear globalization rightly point to the fact that unelected, undemocratic, regulatory bodies now set the framework for global trade and interaction.

A global citizenry is more of an idea than a functioning reality. There is no world government, and few regulatory bodies to which global citizens have access. However, a 'global public opinion' has come into being, and, with it, social movements that see their arena as the whole world rather than the nation–state.

What I have identified as globalization's third wave began with the collapse of Europe's Communist bloc in 1989. After 1989 we can more properly speak of a global world, albeit one in which the major cleavage of East–West has been replaced by the more enduring one of rich and poor. Even so, political globalization in the contemporary world predates the

Communist meltdown. From 1945 to 1989 there had been moves toward international cooperation. In response to the catastrophe of the Second World War, the UN was established in 1945 as a forum of nation–states. The first article of its Charter declares that the primary objective is the maintenance of international peace and security. The UN has played an important role in the maintenance of world peace. Apart from brokering deals, it has also been actively involved. Since 1948, 118 countries have provided more than three-quarters of a million 'peacekeepers' in 54 operations. At the time of the millennium summit, 345,000 personnel were deployed in 15 operations, including longstanding presences in Cyprus and the Golan Heights on the Israel–Syria border, as well as more recent activities in East Timor and Kosovo.

Prior to 1989 the UN could only look on impotently as the world was riven by a bipolar dispute between the US and USSR and their attendant allies. NATO and the Warsaw Pact military alliances effectively meant a divided world. The coordinates of East and West were used to split the world into competing camps. From 1945 to 1989 world politics was dominated by the two power blocs. The respective spheres of influence mapped out the geopolitical force-field of global interaction. There were powerful elements on both sides that had a stake in the continued antagonism. The military–industrial complex of each country promoted the threat of the other in self-serving attempts to bolster continued military build-up and spending. At times a spiral effect was produced as one side saw a fresh threat from the other and responded with new armaments and missiles that, in turn, were seen as intimidatory by the other side. The phrases of military antagonism – 'Missile Gap'; 'Mutually Assured Destruction' (MAD) – dominated a world frozen in a Cold War. The posture of antagonisms petrified social change in both countries. In the USSR, market reforms were too long delayed in comparison with Eastern Europe, hamstrung because of their association with the capitalist enemy. In the US, social reforms that could be negatively represented as 'socialistic' delayed decent welfare provision. The enduring consequences were that Russia, the Ukraine and other areas of the former Soviet Union were unable to move easily into a post-Communist market society, and that the US has still to grant itself welfare provision that would be equivalent to those established by its Western allies. Decent and affordable health care available on demand is still a long way off in one of the richest countries in the world.

The bipolar division structured the whole world. When Lyndon Johnson reputedly said of one Latin American dictator, 'He's a sonuvabitch, but he's our sonuvabitch', he was condensing the imperial role in the Cold War. Leaders and regimes were not assessed and aided in response to the way they treated their own people, but in relation to their alignment with the superpowers. The US was happy to support a sleazebag like Mobutu of Zaire, who looted his country of almost $10 billion, because he was ostensibly anti-Communist. And when friendly elites were crumbling in the face of popular resistance, the superpowers propped them up. Vietnam and Hungary, Czechoslovakia and El Salvador. The US Marines and the Red Army policed their respective spheres of influence. There were also proxy wars and indirect involvement, as with the Cubans in Mozambique or the South Vietnamese in Laos. Internal disputes could be connected to wider geopolitics and the result was an ability by regimes to play external alignment against internal dissension. Dissidents in Eastern Europe and Communists in Latin America could be dismissed as foreign spies rather than be recognized as genuine domestic critics. For at least a generation, meaningful social reform in large parts of the world was icebound in the Cold War's grip.

There were, of course, rises and drops in the geopolitical temperature. In the first phase of the Cold War, the years of 'irreconcilable conflict' from 1947 to 1964, things looked bleak. The two superpowers were squaring up to each other in a steady spiral of armament build-ups. The US was establishing global reach, while the USSR had a more limited ability to influence events beyond its direct sphere of influence. A second phase, a slight thaw into *détente* from 1964 to the late 1970s, was marked by the rhetoric of peaceful coexistence and the growing global reach of the USSR. There was another cold snap, from 1980 to the mid-1980s, when the US, under Reagan's implacable opposition to the USSR and in response to the latter's extending reach, undertook a massive military build-up. There was growing deployment of tactical medium-range missiles by both sides. I remember marching at a huge demonstration in London against the deployment of Cruise missiles in Britain. Many people felt the world was entering a new and dangerous period. The great historian E. P. Thompson, parodying a British Government defence document called *Protect and Survive*, wrote a book entitled *Protest and Survive*.

It ended with not so much a bang as a whimper. It caught most people by surprise. None more than the CIA, whose huge budget and surveillance capacity only allowed them to see the wall, rather than the writing on it. You tend to see what you look for, and, if you are looking for an evil empire, all you will see is the imperialism rather than the internal contradictions. Gorbachev was at least more prescient. His appointment to the presidency in 1985, his commitment to stabilizing the arms build-up and his promotion of *perestroika* and *glasnost* were his realization that the old system needed drastic reform. The fall occurred almost overnight. In 1989 popular protest swept away Communist rule, and this time the Soviets refused to prop up the ailing regimes. Gorbachev refused to lend troops even when requested by the East German leader Erich Honecker. East German protesters chanted *Gorby, Gorby* in public demonstrations. The Soviet refusal to intervene gave the green light to open displays of protest. In the fateful year of 1989:

2 June	Solidarity wins free elections in Poland
19 September	Hungarians set a date for free elections
9 November	The Berlin Wall falls

10 November   Bulgaria's leader is overthrown
24 November   Massive protests in Czechoslovakia end Communist rule
22 December   Ceauşescu's regime in Romania collapses.

When the coup against Gorbachev failed in 1991, it was all over. The resultant break up of the Soviet Union into separate republics and the fall of Communist party power signalled a new world order. A bipolar world had been replaced by what appeared as a single global polity. No longer could repressive regimes appeal to their former geopolitical allies to help maintain the status quo. No longer could the costs of the imperial role be used to delay social reform.

There is no East–West fracture now. The two remaining Communist powers are China, which is about as pro-capitalist as one can get, and Cuba, which seems to serve only as a continual irritant to Cuban exiles and the US Congress. While the whole world does business with China, and the whole world, except the US, does business with Cuba, it is legitimate to speak of a global unity.

While the end of the Cold War inaugurated a new world order, it did not entail a renewed role for the UN. The UN had been ineffective during the Cold War, and even after, because ineffectiveness was built into the UN's design. When the world powers drew up the plans for the previous new world, the power of the UN to act as even an embryonic world government was severely limited. The two main bodies of the UN are the General Assembly and the Security Council. Every country has one vote in the General Assembly, which is a place for general discussion, but in the Security Council, the body responsible for maintaining international peace and security, there were five permanent members – China, France, the UK, the USSR (now the Russian Federation) and the US, as well as six other rotating members that each served for two years. Today the permanent members are the same, but the number of rotating members has been increased to ten. Every country is equal, but some are more equal than others. The two-tier system codifies and reinforces the hierarchy of state power. The great powers dominate the UN.

The UN has played an important role in the creation of a global awareness, but it has not become a centre for world government. This goal has been thwarted by two things. First, the great powers have the most influence within the UN, and successfully resist any form of global government that undermines national sovereignty. Britain supports peacekeeping forces in Cambodia, but was always opposed to having the UN involved in Northern Ireland. The US wants actions imposed on aggressive states, but made its own decision to invade Grenada and Panama. Japan is signatory to species preservation measures, but resists and circumvents bans on whaling. The UN embodies the relative power of different nation–states, it does not transcend them. One measure of national power is the ability to influence UN resolutions. The rich and powerful do not win all the time. Resolutions against the US and their allies have been passed by the General Assembly. Resolutions have been passed about the Israeli handover of the West Bank. But between the resolution and the enactment falls the shadow of the great powers. Not all issues become UN resolutions, and not all resolutions are enacted.

Second, a fundamental tenet of the UN is the principle of national sovereignty. It is built into the charter. All the signatories abide by the article that reads 'The Organization is based on the principle of sovereign equality'. There are self-imposed limits on the ability of the UN to intervene in national domestic issues. There are exceptions to this, to which we will turn presently, but no national government is willing to give up the right to control its own destiny.

The UN has not been incidental to the globalization of the world. But the UN has been most influential in creating a discourse of globalism rather than serving as a centre for world government. If we redefine political globalization to mean a sense of global political connection, then the

UN has become an important element in political globalization. It has been important in a number of discourses that, at the very least, have provided the beginnings of thinking, speaking and acting on global terms. I will briefly mention four.

First, it has aided the process of decolonization. The initial charter spoke of the principle of self-determination. The Trusteeship Council was established to supervise the transition of trust territories (former colonies) to independence. As more of them became independent members of the General Assembly, the Assembly's anti-colonial rhetoric increased. Most of the colonial powers would have been forced to give up their colonies without the UN, for the determining force was armed resistance within the colonies themselves, but the UN's forum provided a steady anti-colonial rhetoric that made it impossible to defend colonial holdings in principle. In practice, Britain, for example, held on to Hong Kong until its treaty with China expired in 1997. However, the General Assembly provided a platform for anti-colonial sentiment that has pervaded the world. No country can justify colonial holdings. An important global principle has been established, and anti-colonialism has become a fundamental tenet of the new world order. We live in a post-colonial world that the UN has helped codify.

Second, the UN has helped in the creation of the notion of universal human rights. In its initial charter the UN spoke of the 'respect for human rights and for fundamental freedoms'. In 1948 the General Assembly proclaimed the Universal Declaration of Human Rights, which enunciated the 'right to life, liberty, nationality, to freedom of thought, conscience and religion'. Since 1989 and the creation of a more unified global polity, the idea of universal human rights has gained more ground. It is a revolutionary idea. The social contract varies from democracy to democracy and in much of the world, until recently, regimes pretty much did what they wanted with their citizens. There was no appeal, no forum, no opportunity to raise a case against the state. The state was the final arbiter, the final court of appeal. In most cases it still is. However, the UN, with its declaration of human rights, its establishment of a Commissioner of Human Rights, an International Court of Justice, also known as the World Court, and an International Law Commission has created a new global framework. Some of the inspiration for all this derives from the Nuremberg trials of Nazi criminals held after the Second World War. The systematic mass murder undertaken by the Nazis was held accountable to universal principles. To be sure, it was the right of the victors. No one was prosecuted for the wanton firebombing of Dresden by Allied bombers, but the Nazis did take inhumanity to new levels. The Nuremberg trials raised the possibility of judging states by international standards. In 1993 the Security Council set up a tribunal to try individuals for war crimes in Yugoslavia. The next year a tribunal was established for genocide in Rwanda, which, in 1998, handed down the first ever verdict of an international court. In 1998 an International Criminal Court was formed to try people for crimes of genocide. In June 2001, the former Yugoslav President, Slobodan Milošević, was arrested and sent to The Hague to await trial on war crimes charges. But we are still at an early stage in the evolution of international law and international accountability.

There is a tension in the UN. One the one hand it is based on the principle of national sovereignty; yet on the other it is upholding the idea of universal human rights and some form of punishment, retribution or at least condemnation of states that transgress those rights. As always, power politics is important. It is easier to indict politicians and governments of small powerless states than it is to indict politicians in Washington, DC, for their conduct of the Vietnam War, or British politicians for army operations in Northern Ireland. It is easier to indict Saddam Hussein or Radan Karavitch than Robert McNamara or Richard Nixon. Even though it is filtered through this grid of power politics, the new discourse and its attendant court and laws is groping toward some codification of international law. It has provided an important standard by which we can assess the treatment of citizens by their governments. Systematic mistreatment, if represented in the world's media by dramatic photos, can animate public opinion, and this raw pressure now has a channel. It is not automatic. The UN is loathe to get involved in domestic issues, and few countries willingly bow to UN condemnation. To be successful, international condemnation has to be backed up by action, otherwise it remains meaningless rhetoric. We can compare what happened in East Timor with Kuwait. Indonesia invaded East Timor in 1975 and received little condemnation and no international response. The 1990 invasion of Kuwait by Iraq was quickly condemned, and troops from an international force, headed by the US, quickly routed the Iraqis. Kuwait is not simply an ally, it is a country with huge oil reserves vital to the US. East Timor had no oil. The UN only got actively involved in East Timor in 2000, when Indonesia-backed militia went on a killing spree. At the time of the millennium summit, three UN aid workers were murdered by militiamen loyal to Indonesia.

It is not that systematic repression equals UN intervention. There needs to be media coverage, and that coverage mustn't undermine the strength of one of the major powers in the country. And even when those conditions are met, there are still enormous questions over the legitimacy, goals, tactics and exit strategies of UN interventions.

Third, environmental issues have been globalized. Issues of environmental quality are clearly global issues. While one country can have stringent clean-air legislation, the fact that other countries still burn fossil fuels or use PCBs, undermines their policy. In the one world we live in, pollution in a single country affects everyone else's air quality. The question of clean air and the ozone layer are issues that can only be dealt with through international negotiation. It is here that the UN has played a role. The Economic and Social Council of the UN has established the UN Environmental Programme (UNEP), which has convened a number of conferences on the thinning of the ozone layer. The UN has been most successful in shifting the debate towards a global awareness of environmental problems. The 1972 conference in Stockholm established UNEP and developed the environment as a global theme. Another conference in 1987 produced a report, *Our Common Future*, which heightened awareness of the idea of a sustainable development, while the Rio conference in 1992 – the so-called Earth Summit – made connections between environmental and development issues, and restated the need for international environmental law. These conferences have shaped a global debate about environmental issues. The discovery of a thinning of the ozone layer in the mid-1980s reinforced the sense of a global threat and the need for global solutions rather than national policies. The Montreal Protocol in 1987 was influential in getting a ban on the production of chlorofluorocarbons (CFCs). At the UN convention on climate change – the Kyoto Conference of 1997 – binding commitments were required to reduce emissions of carbon dioxide and other greenhouse gases that were leading to global warming. US reactions to the Kyoto Protocol reminds us of the limits of international cooperation. The Clinton administration initially agreed with the binding timetables for emissions, but under pressure from intense lobbying by business and labour unions, George W. Bush has refused to go along with the Kyoto Protocol. The constant shifting between international and national interests is most apparent with the more powerful countries, who can undermine international agreements. However, the fact that the US can be identified as a non-signatory is significant. A country's commitment to global interests can now be identified and measured. We have a global metric for political globalization.

Fourth, the UN, through its various agencies and the pronouncements of the General Assembly, has promoted the idea of development and the goal of eradicating the huge imbalance between rich and poor countries. The discourse of development has emerged as more countries have joined the UN. The weaker and the poorer now have a platform in the General Assembly as well as in the various development agencies connected to the Economic and Social Council. The idea of development has not remained fixed. It emerged in the 1950s and crystallized in the 1960s and early '70s into raising the gross national product through the strategy of funding big export-orientated projects such as roads and dams. The emphasis was on capital-intensive schemes. In the past 25 years there has been a critique of this model. The emphasis on capital-intensive rather than labour-intensive ignores the fact that most poor countries have lots of people but limited capital. Many of the early showpiece projects, such as the giant dams, were ecologically destructive, removed indigenous people and only helped to provide power for a narrow range of export-led industries. The early programmes were a disaster in terms of social justice; they rarely helped the poorest, the most needy. There has been redefinition towards sustainable development. The UN Development Programme (UNDP), which operates in 174 countries, now has sustainable human development as its main priority. The Children's Fund (UNICEF), for example, concentrates on immunization, primary health care, basic nutrition and elementary education. The UN has shifted toward a definition of development that is ecologically sustainable and socially fair, rather than one that just increases aggregate economic growth. The UN programmes do not undermine national sovereignty. UN agencies are charged to work with state and local governments. Often they are pulled into local power structures, and development funds rarely filter down to the poorest. But the UN has helped to create a discourse and practice of development and progress. The UN is not the only organization promoting global development, but it is one of the more visible and most influential.

We can identify two forms of political union: deep and wide. A deep unity binds together separate jurisdictions under a shared national culture and popular legitimacy. Good examples are the federation of states both in Australia and the US (since 1865, at least). A wide unity connects separate jurisdictions in a patchwork that lacks depth and cohesion. The USSR was another good example. The distinction between deep and wide is at the core of disagreement in the European Union between the deep Europeans, such as France, Germany, Belgium and The Netherlands, who want to move towards a meaningful political union, and the wider Europeans, such as Britain and Denmark, who want a looser federation that does not undermine national sovereignty. The UN is an example of a very wide but very shallow political union that is still dominated by the bigger powers. Like all international forums it has self-imposed limits. No state wants to give up its national sovereignty. However, both large and small powers want some form of the UN. For the smaller powers, it gives them a voice and the possibility of influencing world debates. For the larger powers, it provides a sense of global order and control, and it can be used to delegitimize rogue states. It also allows them massively to influence world debates. The ultimate limit on world government is the inability of states to give up their power, and the unwillingness of the bigger powers to share power. However, a global awareness has been aided by the actions and presence of the UN. World government has not been produced, but a sense of global connectivity has. Through international agreements, global discourses and the internationalization of law, a global community has been manufactured.

Global Regulation

Global governance has been most successful in the trend towards economic integration. Again, the roots lie in the past, in the aftermath of the Second World War, when the great powers were drawing up a set of rules and regulations for the new world order. Their aim was to avoid the mistakes of the past. The inter-war Great Depression was seen to have arisen from a lack of international regulation and cooperation. The world market, if left only to the force of national interests, could result in national economic protectionism. It was agreed that national markets needed to be opened up to the benefits of free trade. National protectionism had led to the Great Depression. A new international order was needed to regulate the global economy so that the spiral of protectionism leading to recession and on to more protectionism would not happen again. In 1944 agreements were made at Bretton Woods, a small town in New Hampshire, between delegates from 44 nations. John Maynard Keynes was one of Britain's representatives and one of the main architects of the plan. The delegates agreed to establish the International Monetary Fund (IMF) and the World Bank. The IMF was initially set up to provide monetary and currency stability so as to enhance world trade. Members were expected to declare fixed interest rates. The background was a series of severe devaluations in the inter-war period, a time when Germans went shopping trundling wheelbarrows crammed with paper currency just to buy bread. Because fixed exchange rates could lead to balance of payments problems – a country could be paying more for imports than it was receiving from exports – the IMF was empowered to provide credit to member states. The IMF was a sort of bank that lent money to sustain the fixed exchange rate system. However, fixed exchanges went the way of the dodo. The first devaluation of the dollar, in 1971, heralded a move toward floating rates of exchange. In effect, many countries allowed their currencies to float on the market; the value was based not on some fixed figure, but on what the market was willing to pay for it. The IMF seemed to have been made obsolete, but, by the late 1970s, it had reinvented itself. It now acts more as a vigilant supervisor of a country's economic policies as well as a lender of last resort. IMF lending is well publicized. In 1995 it extended credit of almost $18 billion to Mexico and $6.2 billion to Russia. In the wake of the Asian crisis, it lent $35 billion to Indonesia, Korea and Thailand. Russia received another top-up in 1998 of $20 billion.

The IMF currently has 182 members, including former Eastern bloc countries. Each member country contributes a certain sum of money as a credit deposit. Collectively these deposits provide a pool of money that members can draw on. The IMF acts as an international credit union for states. A country's deposits determine both how much it can draw on ('special drawing rights') and its voting power. The richer the country, the more it can draw on and the more power it wields. By 1998 member states had paid in $193 billion, with the US as the largest single contributor at $35 billion. Since this was 18 per cent of the total quota, the US wields 18 per cent of the votes. The IMF is dominated by the rich countries who contribute most and who get to set the agenda through their voting power.

The IMF exercises its power through its system of 'surveillance' (the term the IMF uses) and the strings it attaches to lending. Surveillance involves monitoring of a member's economic policies and evaluation of their economy. IMF surveillance has been strengthened since the Mexican and Asian crises of the 1990s. The IMF has a neo-liberal agenda in which investment is directed to export-driven sectors. The IMF evaluates countries less in terms of their domestic policies and how they treat their citizens, and more in terms of them as efficient cogs in a global economic system. Its claims that it does not get involved in the domestic policies of member countries are fatuous. The IMF promotes neo-liberal economic policies.

IMF lending comes with strings. Borrowing countries must undertake reforms that eradicate economic difficulties and 'prepare the ground for high-quality economic growth'. The reforms are generally devoted to reducing government expenditure, tightening monetary policy and the privatization of public enterprises. The effects of IMF reforms are obvious. In the short to medium term they lead to increased unemployment, reduced social welfare spending and declining living standards for medium to low income groups. IMF discipline is felt most by the weakest groups in a society. The IMF operates to stifle innovative social welfare programmes and redistributive policies. IMF policies work against social justice.

One example of this is South Korea. On 21 November 1997, South Korea asked for IMF assistance in the wake of depleted foreign reserves and rising short-term loans. The IMF agreed to lend $56 billion, and, in exchange, asked for an economic adjustment package that depressed economic growth, caused unemployment, cut government spending, led to a decline in living standards and gave more access to foreign financial institutions. The IMF imposed market principles and a less-regulated international trade on Korean society. The IMF's argument was that South Korea's problems were due to lack of transparency in financial dealings, a bloated public sector and a job market that ensured employment rather than productivity.

IMF lending has been subject to two sorts of criticism. The first has been concentrated on their regressive consequences. IMF lending requirements hurt the poor and punish the weak. A second source of criticism has been its ineffectiveness. IMF lending tends to underwrite bad investment decisions. IMF lending, in effect, pays for the poor choices and decisions of rich elites in Third World countries. While investors' returns are assured, there seems little that the IMF can do to structurally readjust the economic arrangements. The first criticism says the IMF hurts the weakest, the second notes that it does not penalize the corrupt elite. Both are correct. The IMF is not the only bad guy in this scenario. The IMF does not create the inequalities that exist within countries, but it does reinforce them. It does not make corrupt elites, but it seems to bail them out. It is national governments who ask for money from the IMF; the IMF does not force countries to take their loans. And sometimes the IMF is a useful scapegoat used by national governments making unpopular decisions. The South Korean government would probably have had to make structural readjustment without the IMF. With the IMF, criticism was displaced away from the national government towards the foreign Other in an outburst of xenophobia. The citizens of South Korea were happy with globalization when it was assuring economic growth and generating rising employment and living standards. That was the result of Korean ingenuity and hard work. But when the globalization roller-coaster took a dive, it was the foreigners, and the IMF in particular, who were to blame. Globalization is embraced when things are doing well, but censured when things get bad.

The IMF has been criticized from two directions. Complaint has come from broad-based social groups who have demonstrated in the streets. The second has come mainly from the US Congress, the single biggest contributor to the Fund, which believes that the IMF was bailing out incompetent and corrupt elites.

The World Bank was also established at Bretton Woods in 1944. It's initial name, the International Bank for Reconstruction and Development (IBRD) describes its role. It was a fund established to aid the reconstruction of Europe and its first loan was $250 million to a war-damaged France. Once Europe got back on its feet, the Bank widened its remit. Until 1989 it was part of the bipolar world, with funds primarily allocated to increase development to countries allied to the US. Funds went to big capital-intensive programmes. The first loan to a developing country was $13.5 million given to Chile in 1948 for a hydro-electric scheme. In the early 1950s Japan was a major recipient of World Bank loans. The loans in the early years follow a pattern of lending to US allies for large set-piece capital investment for hydro-electric power and transportation projects. There was little monitoring or accountability. Much of the funding was a failure even in its own limited terms of raising aggregate economic growth.

The Bank now has five distinct parts. The IBRD provides market-based loans to middle-income countries. The International Development Assistance, established in 1960, gives interest-free loans to low-income countries. The International Finance Corporation, set up in 1956, provides loans to private investors setting up business ventures in developing countries, and the Multilateral Investment Guarantee Agency underwrites private investment in developing countries. The fifth is an international centre for settling investment disputes.

The World Bank now has almost universal membership, but, like the IMF, it was and still is dominated by the rich members. Five countries –

France, Germany, Japan, the UK and the US – each appoint Executive Directors, while the other countries together appoint nineteen of them. By long-standing agreement, the head of the Bank is an American, while the head of the IMF is a European. Like the IMF, the Bank's headquarters is in Washington, DC, just a few blocks from the White House.

Having little oversight or accountability, the World Bank became known for its inefficiency and for the aid it gave to rich investors and corrupt elites. In response to criticism, both internal and external, from both the developing and developed world, from both private investors angry with delays and administrative chaos and aid workers upset at the corruption and inefficiency, it has shifted its emphasis to eradicating world poverty with more carefully assessed and monitored development schemes. It still operates within closed chambers with little input from the outside, a self-referential system that has come under increasing attack as an elite club dictating regulations in secret meetings. However, the focus of the Bank has changed towards a more accountable, local-scale, global development agency. And through its work and publications, especially the annual *World Development Report*, first published in 1978, the Bank has helped to create a global community.

The World Trade Organization (WTO) is the latest version of what was originally called GATT (the General Agreement on Tariffs and Trade). GATT was established in 1948 as a forum for stimulating world trade by reducing customs duties and lowering trade barriers. Like the IMF and World Bank, it was established with an eye to avoiding the mistakes of the inter-war era, when rising protectionism was part of the cause of the Great Depression. GATT was a forum for getting rid of protectionism. The first round of multilateral discussions, held between 1948 and 1967, led to some tariff reductions. The long drawn-out nature of the discussions led many commentators to suggest that the acronym stood for General Agreement to Talk and Talk. The most decisive round was the Uruguay round, 1986 to 1994, which established new rules for trade in services and intellectual property, new forms of dispute settlement, and trade policy reviews as well as the creation of the WTO in 1995. The WTO now has 138 members, which together account for 90 per cent of the world's trade. China became a full member in 2000. WTO representation now includes ministers. The first ministerial conference took place in 1996 in Singapore, the second in 1998 in Geneva and the third in 1999 in Seattle. The WTO acts as a form of world trade court. In March 1999, 167 cases were brought to the WTO by member countries complaining of unfair trade practices. The WTO also, like the IMF, scrutinizes the trade policy of the individual members.

Like the IMF, the WTO has a neo-liberal agenda committed to free trade and limited protectionism. While all members agree to this in principle, it has been difficult to work through in practice. Free trade is a great idea in principle, and in the long run. But in the long term, as the architect of global regulation, John Maynard Keynes, noted, we are all dead. It is in the short to medium term that we lead our lives. Some economists argue that only a free trade in goods and services around the world will ensure economic growth. In the short to medium term, and that is the dominant phase for most of us this side of political reality, governments have to protect the investments and jobs of domestic industries. Free trade sounds great in the international forum, but try telling that to constituents who are about to lose their jobs or investors about to lose their returns. Every country has certain protected industries, in many cases agriculture, whose protection is necessary for governments wishing to stay in power. Almost all the WTO meetings are held in secret. Officials argue that secrecy enables member countries to admit to the political need for protection and allows the WTO to play the role of a global heavy reinforcing a global discipline, which indeed it does.

Most countries want to be in the WTO, they all want the benefits of world trade, but each has its own national interests. The biggest structural cleavage is between the rich and poor countries. Many of the poorer ones want to protect their fledgling industries from the more efficient competition overseas. They want access to global markets for their goods, but fear that their economies could be assaulted if foreign competition was given easy entry. The Seattle ministerial round was broken up not only by demonstrators but by delegates from developing countries, who refused to go along with the agreements worked out by the richer countries.

Membership of the WTO is vital to countries seeking access to global markets. But this access comes at a price. For the stronger economies free trade can mean access to new markets, especially for banking and intellectual property rights, but it can also mean the decline of traditional industries. For the weaker economies, membership of WTO signifies access to the large consumer markets of the rich world, but can mean an inability to control the fate of traditionally protected industries. Membership of WTO implies a willingness to shape national economic policy around the principle of free global trade.

The WTO seems to have limited environmental sensitivity, in one celebrated case overturning national legislation that had banned the import of tuna caught in nets that killed dolphins: this positive environmental act was seen as a restriction of free trade. The WTO seems unconcerned with working conditions and living standards. The fact that free trade may result in the import or export of goods produced under slave-like circumstances, with children working long hours in dangerous conditions, is not a point that the WTO considers. Yet free trade should not mean free reign. We need to extend our definitions and criterion. Free trade is a simple goal, too simple. Consideration must be paid to what is being traded, who made it, grew it, fished it, and under what conditions. Common humanity demands that we extend our systems of global regulation to encompass a more humane conception of international trade and commerce.

The Nation-State

One simple model of globalization shows nation–states becoming less relevant. Globalization equals the death of the nation–state is a popular image. The death of the nation–state is a compelling and powerful thesis, simple and clear idea. Unfortunately, it is incorrect. Things are rarely so simple or so clear.

Let us begin with an important point. Nation–states have always had an international dimension. They were founded in relation to other states – the word *national* is embedded in inter*national*. The *inter* implies some form of connection between nationals; there is no such thing as an independent national, free from the inters. Nation–states have always existed as international phenomena: they are only legitimized if other states recognize them; they have borders with other countries, they trade with other countries. The 'globalization leads to death of the nation–state' idea, supposes that a nation–state can operate in a vacuum. The very organization of a state is built around its international connections: state departments, foreign offices, defence and war departments, departments of trade and commerce, secretaries of state and foreign ministers, ambassadors and embassies. The international is part of the national. The nation–state is internationalized by its very nature.

But what about the growth of supra-national organizations such as the IMF, World Bank and WTO. Are these not undermining the power of the nation–state? Yes and no. Yes, in the sense these organizations reinforce the *inter* side of the national. Nation–states now operate in a system of global regulation. Domestic policies are now more clearly hedged in by international regulations. The independent power of the state to operate outside these limits is severely constrained. In order to benefit from global trade, you need to be part of the global trade regulatory system, which may impose limits and boundaries to domestic policy making. But *no* because the location of the state in this new global grid reinforces certain elements of the nation–states. The trade departments, central banks and finance departments, for example, of governments are now charged with implementing international regulations. The nation–state is surviving, with certain sections even prospering.

Globalization does tend to reinforce the logic of the market. Free trade, floating exchange rates, open economies and global competition are all aspects of globalization, but the functions and bureaucracies of the states that implement these strategies are strengthened and reinforced. It is not the case that the nation–state as a whole is being undermined by globalization. While rapid capital flows do place limitations on the independent power of the state to influence economic forces, the state still retains immense power in regulating flows of people. While capital is made less restricted by national boundaries, labour is made more controlled. The regulation of immigration is a key function of the state, a role that has been increased and its profile raised. The power of the state to limit flows of people across national boundaries, a fundamental element in national sovereignty, is being increased partly as a response to the xenophobic fears of globalization, and partly from the threat of cheaper labour undermining the wages and conditions of its citizens. The distinction between aliens and guests, visitors and immigrants, citizens and non-citizens is being strengthened.

Globalization does raise issues of scale. Throughout most of the nineteenth and twentieth centuries the nation–state was the scale for emancipation movements. There were *national* liberation movements, there was *national* socialism. It was always national. However, we can legitimately ask this question: Is the nation–state the right scale for life in the new millennium? In an era of global flows of capital and an integrated world economy, the nation–state appears too small to influence economic events. The global economy has weakened its power. Some states are less powerful than others – the US can influence economic trends more easily than Botswana – but even the largest states react to, rather than create, global flows of capital. Global capitalism knows no national boundaries. There is also a whole range of problems that transcend national borders. The ozone level, poverty, hunger, human rights, are all global rather than specifically national concerns. States on their own cannot solve these problems. In many ways the nation–state appears too small for a global world. The paradox is that the nation–state is also too large. It is too small to address global issues, yet too big to respond to local concerns. The state is too parochial for a global community, yet too large for local communities.

Many theorists worry that globalization has or will undermine national sovereignty. Is that such a problem? Those who worry posit a more benign nation–state against an uncaring globalism. This is not always so. Nation–states can oppress their populations. NATO's involvement in Kosovo and UN interventions in East Timor were undertaken because government regimes were terrorizing local populations. In both cases the eventual result was an effective and humane alliance of the local and global against the viciously national. Simply to pose global against national, as the Death of the Nation–State theorists tend to do, is to miss this tripartite scale, in which the only hope for state-oppressed local communities is to mobilize the global.

The simple idea of the nation–state as it is embodied in the Fear of Globalization argument assumes a unified territory. However, we can consider the issues of nation versus state and the development of the city state. A distinction can be drawn between a nation and a state. A nation is a community of people with a common identity, shared cultural values and an attachment to a particular territory. The state is a political organization covering a particular territory. The nation is a group of people, the state is a territorial unit of political organization. There is no simple relationship between nation and state. There are nations without states, such as the Kurds, the Palestinians and the Basques. Many states have more than one nation. Even a long-established democratic state such as the UK contains four nations – English, Scots, Welsh and Irish. While globalization may be undermining the nation–state, globalization may aid nations against states. Nations without states may have no forum apart from international organizations. Nations being repressed by their states can appeal to international standards of human rights. Globalization may be undermining the power of states, but it can also help in the defence of nations. It was international intervention that saved the Kosovars from Serbian oppression. The Kurds continue to survive precariously in northern Iraq because of international forces. Around the world indigenous peoples depend on international public opinion in order to survive or subsist in the face of national indifference. Globalization can help nations survive their states.

The territorial unity of nation–states is being undermined by changes in national policies as well as global trends. The encouragement of the free market and the decline of the Keynsian states are leading to marked regional inequality and difference. In many countries the difference between urban and rural, big city and small town, expanding and declining economies is reinforced by the lack of national equalization policies. The 'national' economy is something of a statistical fiction, an averaging of different urban regions. Economic globalization is aiding the creation of city–states within different countries. Sydney, for example, is developing as Australia's global city. Its appearance and the life experiences of its citizens are becoming more like those found in San Francisco, London and New York than those in the Outback or small-town Australia. Sydney's ability to reposition itself in the global economy allows it to become discrete from the rest of the country. Globalization is aiding the creation of city–states, the control points of a global economy. Globalization is not so much undermining the nation–state as restructuring it. The nation–state is being redifferentiated according to its success in attracting global capital. The nation is being differentiated by globalization. Certain parts are becoming more successful, others less so. In effect, the nation–state is being broken up into degrees of connection with the global economy. In the wake of a widespread withdrawal of state intervention, the result is an increasing difference within the nation–states and a growing likeness between similarly placed urban regions and cities in different countries.

There are complex interactions between the global, national and local that the simple thesis of 'globalization undermining the nation–state' simply fails to comprehend. Let me give an example that condenses a more nuanced model of global–national–local connections. In 1972, at the UN Educational, Scientific and Cultural Organization (UNESCO) general conference in Paris, a number of delegates addressed the problem of threats to the world's cultural and natural heritage. Noting that 'the deterioration or disappearance of any item of the cultural and natural heritage constitutes an harmful impoverishment of the heritage of all nations of the world', the delegates created the World Heritage Convention (WHC), which established a list of sites to be protected. These included Stonehenge (UK), the Galapagos Islands (Ecuador), Machu Picchu (Peru) and Auschwitz (Poland). By 2000 there were more than 630 heritage sites in 118 countries. The list and the process of listing has created a global discourse of cultural and environmental preservation. The WHC has limited power, but it has created a global debate. It is a debate that captures the local, the global and the national. Take the case of Kakadu National Park in Australia, which became a World Heritage Area in 1981. Kakadu is home to the Mirrar people, as well as being the site of one of the richest uranium deposits in the world. The Australian government's decision to allow uranium mining at Jabiluka, close to Kakadu, has aroused the resistance of environmental groups as well as most of the Mirrar. This coalition of Green and indigenous movements has lobbied the WHC to get Kakadu on its danger list as one way of raising international awareness of an 'internationally' important site, and of bringing international pressure on the Australian government.

The WHC is also involved in national issues. By getting sites listed, it raises their international profile, and, in turn, enhances the profile of specific countries. Listing the Borobudur temple in Yogyakarta, Indonesia, increased the number of visiting foreign tourists. The Indonesian government was keen to get the international endorsement of the WHC.

The WHC also publishes a danger list. Australia's Great Barrier Reef was added to the list in 1993, and again in 1994, as local environmental groups brought attention to the possible effects of large tourist developments. When Delphi in Greece was being nominated, the WHC suggested to the Greek government that plans to build an aluminium plant nearby should be reconsidered. The plant was built elsewhere and Delphi was listed. The global community worked with local groups to effect national decisions.

The Cambodian government was very keen to obtain world heritage listing for the ancient monumental city of Angkor Wat. Emerging from 20 years of civil war and social upheaval, the Cambodian government was eager to get international help in the nominating process because it received assistance in developing a management plan and in stimulating international concern and tourist dollars. World Heritage listing dovetailed with national policies.

Some argue that globalization is undermining the power of the nation–state. The World Heritage listings show a more complex story. Nation–states use the World Heritage listing, as do local communities, battling against their national governments. The connections between global, national and local are rich and varied.

A Global Citizenry

'If a man be gracious and courteous to strangers', noted Francis Bacon in 1625, 'he is a citizen of the world'. While it is a common conceit of writers, world citizenship is more of an affectation than a reality. There are no passports to be had for citizens of the world. Try to get into a country by telling the immigration officials that you are a citizen of the world and see how long it takes. But while the practice of world citizenship is wholly undeveloped, the notion of world citizenry has been gaining ground. A number of elements are important. First, there has been the development of a global discourse of human rights, environmental protection and shared projects of poverty reduction. A global vision is emerging. The globalization of the globalization discourse has led to a sense that we are living in one world with shared concerns and interests. The thinning of the ozone layer is a case for concern that involves us as inhabitants of the planet. These global concerns create a globalizing tendency. Some are more immediate than others. Approaching environmental disaster is a more potent force than a longer–term, more distant concern with poverty reduction in faraway lands.

There has not been a steady increase in all aspects of global awareness. The decline of the Cold War has also lessened the global awareness of nuclear disaster. When Mutually Assured Destruction was a possibility there was an international peace movement. This has been difficult to mobilize for more complex issues of nuclear proliferation and the danger of chemical weapons.

In recent years a global consciousness has been reinforced, created and embodied by images of the global. The literal image of one world is a recent phenomenon. Photos of the globe as seen from outer space were unavailable before 1969. The state of the art technology gave us, for the first time, a photographic image of one world, a shared planet. Soon after, in April 1970, Earth Day was established as a worldwide festival of one world environmentalism.

Our view of the world is also shaped by the means of communication. When we are limited by word of mouth, our horizons are limited to the very local. But with the evolution of print, messages can be carried further, communities of readers are extended across space and time. With the electronic media, communities of viewers and listeners can stretch around the world, creating a global community. The global is brought into our living-rooms. Events happening around the world can be viewed as they happen, indeed they can happen because they are on TV. In 1964 Marshall McLuhan referred to the developing 'global village'. I see it more as an occasional global village. Certain events are dramatized. The fall of Milošević in Belgrade in the autumn of 2000 was seen around the world. With mass-media there is now more immediacy to our experience of distant events. There is a new force in world affairs – global public opinion that can be mobilized to release prisoners, undermine governments, legitimize opposition movements, send aid to starving people. There is always the danger of compassion fatigue, as yet more images of starving babies become easier to ignore. But global public opinion, fickle and changeable, ephemeral and unfocused, is now a fact of life. It is one of the more positive aspects of political globalization. When East Germans demonstrated in Leipzig in 1989 against Communist rule, their resistance was seen all over the world and it gave hope and confidence to dissidents in Czechoslovakia and Romania. It is unlikely Nelson Mandela would ever have been released without the unblinking gaze of the world on South Africa. And who knows what might have happened in East Timor if the violence of the militiamen had not been broadcast around the world?

The image of the global, the creation of global public opinion through mass-media, the time–space compression of telecommunications and transport improvements that have brought the world much closer together, have all created the preconditions of global citizenry. However, our sense of who we are is shaped primarily by local and national communities. Global images occasionally flit past us, but the everyday fabric of our lives is still fundamentally shaped by our national location. Who we are is still very much a function of where we are. We read the national press, watch national TV, the education system is in large part an ideological exercise in national consciousness. One of our most important documents when travelling the world is the passport: it denotes our citizenship, our identity and our ability to cross borders. We are still very much stamped by the imprint of the national. A global consciousness has to develop under the heavy impress of the national. The amazing thing is that it has developed at all.

There is the global consciousness of the transnational business class – the international bureaucrat or the conference-hopping intellectual who knows a good tailor in Hong Kong, the most convenient hotel in Kuala Lumpur and where to find the best bagels in New York. The business-class travelling sophisticates have a global perspective from the best suite in a luxury hotel. This is unlikely to produce a fertile area for emancipatory projects. Generating global citizenship on a mass scale for emancipatory social projects is difficult. Global citizenship has few outlets of expression. As citizens we vote for local and national politicians. In Europe people also now vote for Euro-politicians, but, in most places, the extent of our active citizenry stops at the national border. While private capital flows freely, and unelected regulatory bodies such as the IMF and the WTO set global rules, our citizenship of the world is given few ways to express itself. We only vote indirectly for the people who represent us at the UN. So far, globalization has been dominated by private and bureaucratic interests, it has not been subject to the will of the people, with all the compromises and pitfalls that democracy involves. A major agenda item for the new millennium is the democratization of globalization.

At the same time as the millennium summit took place in New York in September 1999, there was a meeting in Prague of the IMF and World Bank. The meetings were also the scene of demonstrations as a motley collection of activists protested against the policies of both organizations. This was not the first public demonstration against the institutions of global regulation. One of the most significant had occurred almost a year earlier, in Seattle.

The WTO held a ministerial meeting in Seattle in November and December 1999 to launch a new round of trade liberalization talks. Over 135 countries were represented. The event seemed to galvanize a wide body of opinion. Almost 1,200 non-government organizations in 87 countries signed a petition calling for a fundamental reform of the WTO. Groups as varied as the Self Development of Indigenous People in Mexico and the Friends of the Earth joined common cause to condemn the present system of world trade and the closed and regressive nature of WTO rules and regulations. The planning of such groups as the Direct Action Network organized effective public protest.[6] On Tuesday 30 November the official opening of the conference was delayed as almost 20,000 people blocked the delegates entering the meeting at the Washington State Convention and Trade Centre and effectively closed down the centre of the city. Over the next few days protest actions were seen around the world, and the WTO, which had been an organization unknown to the wider public, was pushed into the harsh glare of media attention. The next day estimates of the crowds had increased to 50,000. While images of property damage were widely broadcast (the destruction of a Starbucks coffee-shop was given coverage in many newspapers), the demonstrations succeeded in shifting public opinion towards a closer scrutiny of the WTO and the supposed benefits of free trade. The complaints widened to a critique of consumerist society, declining environmental quality and the power of multinationals. The WTO was put on the defensive. The talks were essentially cancelled not only because of the protest, but also because the delegates could not sign off on an agreement. Many delegates from developing countries were buttressed in their concerns by the 50,000 protesters.

The protests had raised the issue of the WTO. Even the business press took up the issue. A few days after the Seattle debacle, a business trade journal noted that

> the peaceful protests underlined an undeniable current of public sentiment. In part, it's worry about jobs and personal futures in an era of great change. In part, it's ignorance about the benefits of

trade. And in part, it's concern over specific issues like labour rights and environmental protection... Another point that's clear from the Seattle fiasco is that the WTO needs to be more open, both externally and internally. One of the reasons for the dark public paranoia about the WTO is that, even if they want to, people can't find out much about how it works as it works. One of the reasons developing countries were upset during the ministerial meeting is that they could find out little about what was happening behind the scenes.[7]

The success of Seattle led to plans for protests at the joint IMF/World Bank meeting in Washington, DC, on 16–17 April 2000. Estimates of the number of demonstrators varied from 35,000 (according to the organizers) and 10,000 (according to the police). Whatever their number, they succeeded in closing down the city and drawing public attention to both organizations. The meetings went ahead and the police, learning from the Seattle experience, successfully managed to get delegates to the meetings. More than 1,500 officers in riot gear handled the protesters with varying degrees of consideration. However, the institutions responded to the criticism. Although he disagreed with their methods, one delegate, the Argentine treasury secretary, noted that 'I think the protesters perhaps have some points'. On 16 April the IMF issued a communiqué that acknowledged the growing discontent with globalization and that prosperity was not reaching everyone. The IMF announced new initiatives to place a renewed emphasis on debt relief for poorer nations and tighter auditing of IMF loans to avoid abuse. Even the US Treasury Secretary, Lawrence Summers, observed at the meeting that there was a gap between the Bank's policies and actual results. The next day it issued a statement pledging more money to fight AIDS, and speeding up debt relief for developing nations. The Bank's president, James Wolfensohn, claimed it was focusing its energies on small-scale programmes aimed at eradicating poverty.

Prague, Seattle, Washington, DC. They represented many things, but for me one of the most telling is that they signalled the beginnings of an international civil society. Civil society is the public space between and beyond and outside formal political arrangements. They are the neighbourhoods groups, the soccer clubs, the carpools, the ties that bind us in informal connections. Many decry the diminishment of civil society, the decline of civic virtues and community involvement – what Robert Putnam has described as 'bowling alone'. However, what Prague, Seattle and Washington, DC, showed was the radical edge of the beginning of an international civil society. There are others. Twinning arrangements between cities that move beyond exchanges of political dignitaries is just one of the connections that link real people in different places in shared communities of interest.

Political globalization has been primarily concerned so far with the organization of rules that emphasize free trade, deregulation and privatization, and favour corporate capital rather than labour interests and the environment. However, events and connections in the three cities showed us the beginnings of a civil society that is as much international and cosmopolitan as national and parochial. It is difficult to sustain. Our strongest communities tend to be the ones where face-to-face contact is maintained at regular intervals in sustained connections. But the internet, cheaper travel and, above all, a shared sense of global citizenry is slowly emerging. So far it is most obvious in the case of protest. But it has to start somewhere. Subsequent political globalization should be concerned with how we create an international civil society that is open and fair and democratic, and provides a balance to the power of the rich and the powerful. Globalization is feared because it is not subject to public debate and public scrutiny. Globalization is endured and experienced, not controlled or managed. The internationalization of political discourse is only just emerging as a subject of citizen involvement and engagement.

When asked where he came from, the Greek philosopher Diogenes said 'I am a citizen of the world'. The Stoics argued that each of us lives in two communities: the local community of our birth and the broader global community of human reason and aspiration. Global citizenship was not lauded as superior to local connections, but existed to reinforce and strengthen them. The pulls of patriotism are many compared to the fragmentary, ill-defined benefits of cosmopolitanism. And yet when we recognize our moral commitments to the global community and extend the ideas of national community to an international community, then, and only then, will a real and meaningful political globalization take place. It is only within an international civil society, with engaged global citizens and a global moral consciousness, that political globalization can live up to the emancipatory promise suggested by the one-worlders.

A global citizenry, a global humanism. Easy to write, difficult to create. But if globalization is to be more than a corporate con-trick, then an international civil society has to theorized, nurtured, sustained and promoted.

Let me close this chapter with an example of good globalization, a case where a combination of international civil society, international organizations and nation–states combined to produce good things. In 1990 Rotary International gave $230 million for the eradication of polio. Polio is now a disease of poor countries that primarily affects children. The Rotary is organized locally in branches around the world. It is an example of international civil society, with no explicit political or ideological position. It joined forces with the World Health Organization to eradicate polio by the year 2000. Together they worked with health departments in countries around the world. The nation–state was not undermined by globalization, Departments of Health were strengthened in their domestic arena by the international promise of money and help. In 1995 in the Middle East, 19 countries held national immunization days. In 1997 some 181 million children were immunized in one week in South Asia. By 1997 over 450 million children around the world had been immunized against polio – three-quarters of all children in the world aged under five. The number of cases of polio reported globally has fallen drastically and the disease will probably be eradicated from the face of the earth by the year 2005. That is a wonderful achievement that was made possible by a global programme, global consciousness, global humanism, international civil society and nation–states. Globalization comes in many shapes and forms. Not all of them are dark and sinister.

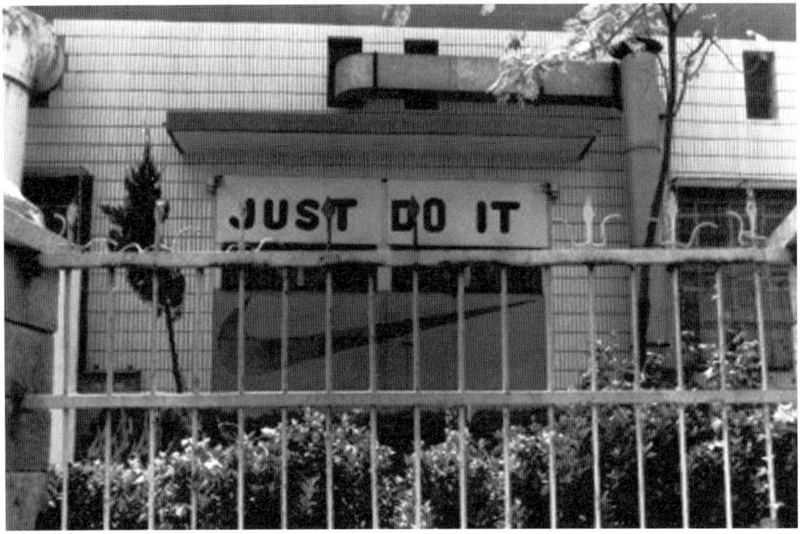
JUST DO IT

CHAPTER FOUR

A Global Economy?

An image and a story. *The image*: the Nike swoosh. We have all seen it. It is one of those ubiquitous images that is both readily recognizable and instantly forgettable. We see it so often we scarcely notice it. We see it and we do not see it. *The story*, recent, but half-remembered, half-forgotten: in February 1995 one of Britain's oldest merchant banks, Barings, collapsed. The main reason was the losses that amounted to almost $1.4 billion, incurred by a 28-year-old trader, Nick Leeson, who was manager of Barings' futures trading unit in Singapore. He lost the money in speculative trading on the Japanese stock market. The media presented it as a cautionary tale of rogue traders and speculative investing. But was it really the unavoidable result of a largely unregulated global financial market?

The image and the story tell us much about two important elements of economic globalization. The Nike image embodies the globalization of production and consumption. The Barings story reminds us of the process of financial globalization.

Global Production Chains: The Swoosh Made Around the World

The North-West US is clearly an important place for globalization. The story of Nike, as well as those of Starbucks, Eddie Bauer, Microsoft and grunge rock, begins in the Pacific North-West.

At the tail end of the 1950s Phil Knight was a member of the University of Oregon track team. He once ran a 4.13 minutes mile. His coach was the legendary Bill Bowerman, who had been at Oregon since 1947. Bowerman was obsessed with performance improvement. He would mix up vats of tar to lay down on running tracks to make them all-weather surfaces. And he would put rubber on waffle irons to make soles for running shoes. Bowerman did not believe that the German-made Adidas, then the shoes of choice for most serious runners, were good enough or cheap enough.

Knight went on to Stanford Business School and, when faced with a term paper, he developed the idea that low-cost Japanese shoes could find a market niche in the US athletic shoe market. He did not pursue the idea immediately, he became an accountant in Oregon; but on a trip to Japan in 1963 he picked up a pair of Tiger running shoes. He showed them to Bowerman, who thought they were better than Adidas shoes. They invested $1,000 in a thousand pairs of Tiger shoes and sold them at local high school track meets. It was the beginning of a lucrative connection. Bowerman would send designs to Japan and new shoes would be made, shipped back to Oregon and sold at track events. By 1969 the annual sales were almost $1 million. Knight and Bowerman sold the shoes under the Japanese brand names, but, in 1971, Knight decided it was time for a separate identity. The shoes were named after the Greek goddess of victory, Nike. The swoosh – the fat check-mark symbol – was the invention of a Portland design student in 1972. Annual sales that year were $3.2 million. By 1980 they were $270 million, and one out of every three Americans owned a pair of Nikes. When the stock went public in 1980 Knight's estimated worth was $100 million; by 1993 it was over one billion dollars. By 1998 Nike was making 90 million shoes per year and generating annual revenue of $9.6 billion.

Making shoes is dirty, dangerous and difficult. Initially, Nike shoes were made in Japan. After the Second World War, Japan had started out on a trajectory of rapid growth in manufacturing. They had a reputation for cheap, shoddy goods. I remember as a schoolboy the term 'Japanese' was used to refer to cheap radios that did not work. 'That's Japanese', we would say derogatively. Little did we know what was to come. The Japanese perfected design improvements and the products they sold on the world market got better and better. So did their wages and conditions. Labour costs rose. In 1974 Phil Knight made his first visit to South Korea. By the early 1980s most Nike shoes were made in Korea, and the city of Pusan became the capital of Asian shoe manufacturing. Nike signed contracts with Korean shoe-makers. Factories sprouted up, more workers were employed. South Korea was one of the fastest-growing manufacturing nations in the world. Meanwhile, during the 1970s and 1980s, some 65,000 jobs in shoe manufacturing in the US were lost.

By the mid-1990s a pair of Nike shoes that sold for $30 actually cost around $4.50 to make. Line workers in Korea were receiving $800 a month. But in the competitive shoe business further cost reductions were needed. Nike could reduce their costs by getting their shoes made in China, Indonesia and Vietnam, where labour costs were only $100 a month. In Vietnam in 1998, workers at a Nike factory earned as little as $1.60 a day. In Indonesia, workers were sometimes receiving as little as 50 cents a day. Indonesia is now one of the largest suppliers of Nike shoes: 17 factories employ 90,000 workers producing around 7 million pairs of shoes annually. In South China the centre for shoe manufacture is the city of Guangzhou. Just outside Guangzhou, one shoe factory that Nike uses makes 35,000 pairs a day.

The story of Nike is one that can be found in most manufacturing sectors. In the past 40 years there has been a global shift in manufacturing employment. In the 1950s the bulk of the world's manufacturing jobs were in the old industrial heartlands of North America and Western Europe. This was the result of an international division of labour that had emerged over the previous 200 years. The core of the world economy imported raw materials and then turned them into manufactured goods that were exported around the world. The process was not simply the result of market forces. Imperialism played a role. In the early decades of the nineteenth century, India had a flourishing cottage industry of cotton manufacturing in Dacca. Official British policy was to destroy this industry, thus the duty paid in India for British cotton goods was only 2 per cent, while the British tariff on cotton goods made in India was 10 per cent. Encouragement was also given to stimulate cotton growing; less tax was levied on land given over to cotton. The result was that India became a producer of raw cotton and an importer of cotton goods made in Britain. This pattern was repeated around the world.

This division of labour involved an unequal exchange in which the core economies of Europe and North America got richer. Cheap raw materials rarely provided the basis for industrial take-off at the periphery; but in the core economies, the value added work of manufacturing provided the basis of sustained capital accumulation. It was also the basis for the creation of an organized working class. Throughout Europe and North America, industrial production provided the basis for working-class organization and resistance that ranged from direct political representation to industrial unions and self-help schemes. By the mid-twentieth century, labour was a significant and important factor in the economic and political life of advanced capitalist countries. While they rarely lived up to the revolutionary mission assigned them by Marx and Engels, in some cases a labour aristocracy aligned itself with the imperial venture: they did transform liberal societies into liberal-democratic societies, humanized an ascendant capitalism and wrought major concessions in social policy and welfare provision. The strong labour organizations were the political and economic basis for the Keynsian compromise between capital and labour in the advanced capitalist countries.

There are differences; a continuum from Scandinavian democracies to the US covers most of them. In many European countries a working class-consciousness led to explicitly Left-wing political groupings and a distinctly welfare-ist state. In the US, by contrast, class loyalties were often undercut by ethnic and racial identities; left-wing parties failed to reach political prominence and ideologies of individualism and middle-class status were stronger than communitarian beliefs and working-class consciousness. There was a variety of state interventions that ranged from the full welfare provision of Scandinavia to the lower safety net in the US.

The global shift in manufacturing employment has meant a reconstruction and re-territorialization of the working class. A predominantly male, North American/European working class has been replaced by a young, female, Asian working class. Most of the workers in the Asian shoe industry are young women. The unionized shoe workers of the US, earning union rates, have been replaced by young Asian women. An old, established self-conscious working class has been effectively destroyed, and a new one has yet to crystallize into political and economic power.

The steady decline in union power in the traditional core countries has made it easier for governments to promote free trade and trade relations that further undercut union power. Since the 1970s the global shift in manufacturing employment has also meant a decline in the power of organized labour to promote its agenda. The result has been a strengthening of capital in the ongoing capital–labour struggle. In the new global world, capital can move to cheaper labour areas, while organized labour in traditional manufacturing industries such as textiles and shoe manufacturing has seen the jobs move away. When people criticize globalization, it is this trend they are often referring to: the ability of corporations to move to cheap labour areas in other parts of the world.

When people hear the term globalization, it is this restructuring that they often imagine. This fear of globalization in the richer countries is entirely justified. Globalization means the ability of corporations to relocate in order to minimize wage costs.

There has been a de-territorialization of corporations. The old adage that what is good for General Motors is good for the US no longer applies. Although listed as a US company, Nike's interests do not necessarily parallel US interests. What is good for Nike shareholders is good for Nike shareholders. Whether it is also good for US workers is beside the point. The low cost of international transport and the growing ease of international trade – both crucial requirements for economic globalization – have allowed capital to be more easily dissociated from national interests and local community concerns. Globalization has liberated capital from territory, citizens and communities. Capital moves at will, roaming the world's space in search of lower and lower wages, while those without capital are stuck in place. Space and place; freedom and constraint.

Capital's mobility has been reinforced by changes in production. The standard model of industrial production is often called 'Fordist', after the assembly line techniques devised by Henry Ford, when large factories in fixed locations produced extensive batches of a limited range of goods. You could have a Model T Ford in any colour so long as it was black. Ford cars were made in Ford factories by Ford workers. The plants were huge, fixed capital investments. Bargaining between capital and labour thus took place against a fixed location. More recently a more flexible form of production has been introduced. Nike, for example, has no shoe factories and no Nike workers. Nike's shoes are made under contract by a range of shoe manufacturers. Factories compete to obtain Nike orders, and are then licensed by Nike if they are capable of making shoes to cost and design specifications. Many of the 'Nike' shoe factories in Indonesia and China are owned by Koreans and Taiwanese business interests. This system drives costs and prices down. The old model of manufacturers making things and retailers selling them has been replaced by the power of retailers and brands. Now retailers tell the manufacturers what to produce. Contracts are for short-run lines rather than long-run batches. One clothing retailer, Hennes & Mauritz, a Swedish company with stores in Europe and North America, keeps its prices low by contracting in low-wage areas of the world. Almost 900 factories produce a constantly changing design portfolio. The company has been successful in keeping its inventory low; the just-in-time production system ensures that goods are made to meet demand. Stores often receive daily supplies. The entire inventory is turned over eight times a year; the industry standard is four times. High turnover means that profits can be made through selling many items rather than one; hence the price of individual items can be reduced, which, in turn, aids turnover. Designs seen at Italian fashion shows are produced cheaply and quickly and then sold in stores until the next fashion wave hits. Just-in-time flexible production allows low prices and high turnover. It also means a marked change in capital–labour relations. Capital is now hypermobile. Workers in one factory cannot bargain in the same effective way that the workers of the old Ford system could. Capital is no longer fixed in place. Retailers can move their production contracts to another factory in another country. While capital can roam the world, labour is fixed in place. The result is an uneven bargaining arrangement.

Capital does not have a completely free hand. It is a highly competitive industry. If you are Nike, you have to compete with Adidas and others in a fast-changing market where consumers are always looking for the best deal and the coolest shoes. If you are a shoe manufacturer you have to compete with other factories to win the orders from companies like Nike. If you have a shoe-store you need to provide a wide range of constantly updated shoes at good prices. The intense global competition ultimately leads to better deals for consumers. The system produces the kingdom of consumer sovereignty in which consumers have real choices. Good-quality items are available at competitive prices in much of the rich world. In real terms, the prices of clothing and shoes have decreased. Globalization has worked in the interests of the rich consumers.

What about the workers in the new areas of global manufacturing production? Initially, wages are low – that is why the companies went there in the first place – but in the first wave of newly industrializing countries, such as South Korea, wages did rise. A successful industrial economy grew and a substantial middle class was created. In the current second wave of newly industrializing countries, such as Indonesia, China and Vietnam, the experience has varied. There has been evidence of exploitation. In the 1990s, news reports of wages as low as 20 cents per hour, forced overtime and dreadful working conditions created a movement against sweatshop conditions in Third World countries. Nike has been singled out for some heavy criticism. A report by CBS in 1996 and a one-hour documentary by the sports channel ESPN entitled *Made in Vietnam: The Sneaker Controversy* pointed to Nike's poor record in Vietnam.

In 1992 Nike drafted its first Code of Conduct, which banned the use of forced or child labour and made subcontractors abide by local laws and standards. These were rarely adhered to. Nike workers in Vietnam received $37 per month, while the minimum wage in Vietnam was $45. It was not simply that the wages were low in global terms, they were low even for Vietnam. Other companies did much better by their workers: Reebok was paying workers $67 a month, Coca-Cola paid $80 a month and state enterprises regularly paid $90. Bad publicity made Nike update its Code of Conduct in 1997 to include the right to free association, paying at least the minimum wage and restricting the working week to 60 hours. Global civil society had exercised some leverage on Nike, a company whose success is determined by its public image. The Nike company report in 1998 claimed that they ceased business with eight factories in four countries that did not meet their code of conduct.

Shoe factories and clothing factories provide wages for people in selected areas of certain developing countries. They have to work hard in difficult conditions. So far, they are rarely organized into effective labour organizations. Workers are recruited for short periods of time; there is a large pool of unemployed willing to take the jobs and there is competition from other factories in other parts of the world. Capital can find cheaper and cheaper areas of production. Are there signs of improvement? Shoe manufacturing might be one of those dirty industries that get passed on to the newest industrializing area. They provide the first wave of industrial jobs, a crash course in the ugly side of global capitalism. But workers in Indonesia, Vietnam and China are going to get organized, and, in alliance with social movements in the consuming countries, they will leverage better conditions. There is an emerging nexus of shared interest between the new working class and the consuming class. Large corporations are vulnerable to bad publicity, boycotts, images of them as exploiters of young Asian women. People in the rich world can make this exploitation a source of consumer decision-making. A global humanism can make a difference.

There are those who argue that even the job loss in the old areas and low-paid jobs in the newly industrializing areas are simply short-term readjustments. The process is one of greater efficiency in the longer term. Free trade and low tariffs mean that a global economy is actually working. Globalization leads to lower prices, more efficient operations and rising standards of living over the long term. The intense competition makes manufacturers constantly seek out the most efficient production techniques. If this involves the closure of shoe factories in the US and the opening of new ones in Vietnam and Indonesia, then this works out in the long run to everyone's benefit. Old inefficient industries are closed and there is a more efficient reallocation of capital and labour to more productive sectors and regions. People who grew rice inefficiently can now make shoes efficiently, while those who made shoes inefficiently can now make computers or aeroplanes or movies.

In the long term that sounds great, but we live in the short to medium term. The former shoe-workers are only able to get more efficient jobs if they get the requisite retraining skills. And people cannot simply relocate without emotional distress. To lose your job if you have done it in the same place for many years, a place with friends and connections where you feel a sense of loyalty and belonging, is not a simple economic reallocation. It can be a gut-wrenching, frightening experience that touches the deepest sense of personal worth. If this experience comes under the rubric of 'globalization', it is no wonder that people fear globalization. Reallocation of resources is a human process, not a bloodless economic calculation. It should involve a commitment to retraining and widespread investment in human capital. But what do we do if capital simply does not want to go to certain areas? What do we do with the people and places left behind: the old textiles towns, the declining industrial regions, the empty shoe factories, the abandoned spaces, the black holes of contemporary capitalism? These are questions that the champions of global free trade fail to address, let alone answer. Globalization forces these questions to the front and centre. We need an active debate on the human consequences of a globalized economy. There is a role for international civil society exercising world public opinion to force and maintain changes. There is a war to be won, and it is a struggle over the meaning of our society and our global connections. Shouldn't global humanism look at free trade not as an end in itself, as some kind of economist's holy grail, but as a means to emancipate people around the world from backbreaking poverty and stunted opportunities?

The debate is often polarized into free trade versus protectionism. The division is overlain by the triumphalists for the future versus the pessimists that look back to a cosier world. It is a false choice. There are clearly advantages to be gained from a free trade that allows workers in poor countries to get a living wage and helps alleviate global disparities in income and life chances. A free market provides the opportunity for people in low-wage economies to benefit from global economic growth. Access to the giant markets of the rich countries is a necessary prerequisite for sustained economic growth around the world. There are costs. Some workers in the rich countries will lose their jobs. Some cities and regions will face economic dislocation. In the old industrial areas there will be a political economy of decline, while in the new industrial areas there will be the political economy of growth with resultant environmental pressures and poor working conditions. These are issues that need to be considered, they are not simply short-term dislocations, they are medium- to long-term consequences of global shift. It is not free trade versus protectionism, or even a global economy versus a non-global economy, it is an humane global economy against an inhumane one. The crucial question is how can we, as global citizens, affect a transformation so that the global economy pays heed to social consequences and environmental effects? How can we use the weight of global public opinion and international civil society to effect a truly human globalization?

One consequence of global shift has been the increase in international trade. An increasing share of spending on goods and services is devoted to imports. More and more of the goods we have are made in other countries. The share of international trade in total output rose from 27 to 39 per cent between 1987 and 1997 for developed countries. The corresponding figures for developing countries were 10 and 17 per cent. The production chains of international corporations such as Nike now weave their way through many countries. The empirical evidence suggests that there is a correlation between international trade and per capita income. Less protectionism means greater competition and awareness of new foreign ideas and technologies; for poor countries, it means the ability to import capital equipment necessary for long-term economic growth. The result is more efficient economies. More open trade leads to rising per capita income. However, per capita income is a crude measure that does not measure the distribution of income, simply the average. The evidence on income distribution is inconclusive. There are examples of countries where income inequality actually increased in the wake of trade liberalization: Argentina,

Chile, Colombia, Costa Rica and Uruguay all saw increasing inequality. In the US the wage rates of high school educated males fell by 20 per cent from 1975 to 1995 as the US economy became more open to foreign imports. It is difficult to assess fully the role of trade in this inequality, because technological changes that weaken the position of selected labour groups are also a factor that is difficult to disentangle. However, the perception of rising inequality is apparent, and it is most often associated with foreign trade. In the US, for example, the declining incomes of the middle class are commonly associated with cheap imports, foreign workers, capital disinvestment and reinvestment in cheaper producing areas, and globalization in general.

Liberalizing trade has yet to reduce global disparities. Indeed the disparities have widened. In 1960 the average per capita GDP in the richest 20 countries was 15 times that of the poorest 20. By 2000 the difference was 30 times. Rich countries have got richer, faster. However, poor countries that were more open to global trade got richer than countries that were less so or closed. The system is unfair and inequitable. But to be left out is to be made poorer.

Does opening up to global trade lead to less poverty? The evidence is scanty but does suggest a positive relationship; more openess to international trade leads to an increase in the income of the poor. However, benefits tend to be over the long term, while costs, especially for workers in previously protected industries, are immediate. Opening economies to free trade and trade reform in general needs to be linked to social programmes that act as a safety net for the short-term dislocations, in conjunction with educational and retraining programmes for the longer term. Again, the issue is not free trade versus protectionism, but what kind of free trade? We need a global trade system that pays attention to the human dimension, the social costs and the position of those who are most vulnerable.

A global trading system can lead to a massive redistribution from rich to poor countries. It can also mean the rich in either country get richer and the poor remain much the same, while workers in both groups are simply more exploited as they are forced into competition with each other. Capital gets to move around the world, while labour is stuck in place. Space and place. Freedom and constraint. This is one consequence of globalization, but it need not be the only consequence. Globalization is currently a possibility, not a finished outcome.

Although I have used the term 'economic globalization', it is something of a misnomer. It has been a work in progress rather than an achieved end-point. Not all firms are footloose, and technology transfers between countries remain problematic. A truly global economy would have a free transfer of capital and labour. What we have is free movement of capital while labour is increasingly state regulated. Moreover, not all countries have got involved in the global economy. The so-called 'Asian Tigers', despite recent crises, have dominated the global shifts in production. Japan, Hong Kong, Singapore, South Korea and Taiwan comprised the first wave of newly industrializing countries. More recently, Indonesia, the Philippines and China have attracted the bulk of manufacturing investment. Although we may think of global production chains, in practice only a few countries are involved: Nike's Air Max Penny shoes have 52 components from only five countries – the US, Taiwan, South Korea, Indonesia and Japan. Economic globalization is spotty. Much of sub-Saharan Africa has been excluded from both the first and second waves of new industrialization. A global economy is *becoming* rather than being, and it is selective, patchy and incomplete.

Poverty tends to be worst in those countries that are less connected to the world economy. At the end of the 1990s there were around 1.2 billion people living on less than a one US dollar a day. When we double the figure to just $2 a day, that then covers 2.8 billion, almost half the entire human population. Poverty rates are highest in South Asia and Africa, with close to 50 per cent of the population living below $1 a day. All the evidence suggests that more open trade leads to growing incomes. The incomes may be very unevenly distributed, but poverty reduction tends to come in the wake of economic growth, which is most sustained with open trade. The problem for many people in the world is not the global economy, but that they are so loosely connected to it. Over half of the world's population is living close to poverty not because they are exploited by foreign corporations or because they work in factories making shoes for Nike. Indeed, a case could be made that their best way to avoid poverty would be to work for Nike. While the conditions may not be ideal – and by saying this I am not legitimizing Nike's position – a brutal fact is that the more closed an economy is, the poorer people tend to be. This not does mean a mindless commitment to free trade; rather, it implies that global connectivity is one of the best ways to alleviate global poverty. It is not without dangers and risks, but for many people around the world, economic globalization may be more of a solution than a problem. There are, of course, global connections and global connections. At worst, a country can be involved in global trade that could consist mainly of the export of rich commodities at low prices to foreign companies who repatriate most of the profits, while the local revenue is held in the hands of the elite with little trickle down. Angola and its oil reserves is a case in point. In this case, global trade reinforces the oppression of the people. It is not the root cause. Better prices for the oil, which is what OPEC managed to achieve as far back as the early 1970s, and a more even distribution of income would provide the basis for the alleviation of poverty. Economic globalization is not the answer, but a humanized economic globalization is at least a start to dealing with intractable problems of global hunger, want and poverty.

Global Consumption Communities

The Nike swoosh has become a global icon that is seen and consumed around the world. Global consumption is as much an element of economic globalization as global shifts in production.

Nike promotes its image and its products through a variety of traditional means, including sloganeering (*Just Do It*) and advertising campaigns in the media. Nike also uses sports personalities. In the beginning the emphasis was on American sports personalities: the two-sport (baseball and football) player Bo Jackson was an early advertising vehicle with the slogan *Bo Knows*. But perhaps Nike's most famous athlete has been the basketball star Michael Jordan. The rise of Jordan and Nike went hand in hand. Jordan's success with the Chicago Bulls was matched by Nike's growth. There was a symbiosis between athletic and corporate success that lead to bigger shoe deals for Jordan and more market penetration by Nike.

Athletes became the main vehicle for Nike's advertising, especially when Nike went more global. Perhaps the best example of a global campaign is the Nike relationship with the golfer Tiger Woods. The company signed the three times US amateur champion to a $40 million deal in 1997. It seemed an awful lot of money at the time; in retrospect, it looks like a great bargain for Nike. Woods went on to win the US Masters and then almost every other major championship, including the US and British Open and PGA. His phenomenal golfing skills – not least his ability to win the big championships, his charismatic smile and his multi-ethnic background (his father is part African–American, part Native American; his mother is from Thailand) have given him a global significance in a world market. TV ratings double when Tiger Woods tees off in a game and the sale of Nike golf clothes and equipment has skyrocketed since the original Woods deal. His multi-ethnicity seems tailor-made to appeal to everyone. He has extended golf's appeal from the narrow preserve of middle-aged, middle-class country club types. His appeal is more universal than the usual run of White golfers. Woods, in contrast, exudes charisma. His success attracted other companies. In April 2000, Coca-Cola, in association with American Express, Rolex and Nike, agreed to sponsor the Tiger Woods Foundation. Coke became the official drink at the junior golf clinics run by Woods that were targeted at low-income areas. The Woods Foundation gets sponsorship and Coca-Cola aligns its name with a global superstar. This was new venture for Coca-Cola, who hitherto had rarely sponsored sports stars. However, their rival Pepsi had already signed up the soccer stars David Beckham and Dwight Yorke of Manchester United and Roberto Carlo of Real Madrid.

The hours of TV coverage of Woods winning yet another title always show the trademark swoosh on the front of his ever-present golf-cap. In 2000 Nike and Woods renegotiated their deal; Woods was to be paid $90 million over the next five years. Nike had a one-man global marketing campaign.

Woods is the exception rather than the rule. Few sports personalities reach the global significance that he has achieved. Nike's advertising is both local and global. Nike now sponsors athletes and teams all over the world. The Nike swoosh is given local signification when it is on the shorts and shoes of local and national athletic heroes. Eager to get into the soccer shoes market, Nike now sponsors the Dutch and Brazilian teams as well as a variety of clubs in national leagues around the world. Nike is a good example of *glocalization*. The term refers to a more subtle relationship, when companies simultaneously go local as well as global, using local signifiers to market global products.

Heineken, a good example of a company that has a global product, a beer in easily identifiable green bottles, also has a strategy of buying local breweries and then marketing and exporting beer manufactured in them. Heineken owns and sells Presidente beer from the Dominican Republic and Star beer from Ghana.

But the most famous example of a global company must be McDonald's. The first McDonald's restaurant was opened in 1940 by two brothers, Dick and Mac McDonald, in San Bernadino, California. The first franchise opened in 1954 in Illinois, now a McDonald's museum. McDonald's was first listed on the New York Stock Exchange in 1966. The following year its first restaurants outside the US opened in Canada and Puerto Rico. By 2000 there were 26,000 restaurants in 119 countries.

A global company with a world-wide product, McDonald's has adapted to local circumstances. It insists on fixed standards, menus, formats and styles of eating. It is standardization taken to new heights. All the mystery and variety of eating is transformed into a predictable, unvarying experience, a successful model repeated endlessly around the world. But there are local variations. Tastes are changed for national markets (in Australia the restaurants proudly note that the beef is 100 per cent Australian) and, in a celebrated case, even political allegiances are proclaimed. In March 1999, a McDonald's restaurant in Belgrade was vandalized by angry mobs. Yugoslavia's fifteen McDonald's restaurants were closed as popular resentment against NATO's bombing campaign focused on a recognizable Western icon. But the restaurants soon re-opened with a new local identity. The managing director, Dragoljub Jakic, had quickly pulled together a survival strategy that promoted McDonald's as a Serbian company. They offered a McCountry, a domestic pork burger with paprika garnish, they produced posters and lapel buttons with iconic Golden Arches topped by a traditional Serbian cap and they gave away 3000 free burgers at an anti-NATO rally held in Belgrade. The campaign was a product of local management neither directed nor encouraged by the head office in Oak Brook, Illinois. After the war was over, McDonald's prospered. As one teenage Serbian noted, 'I don't associate McDonald's with America. Mac is ours.'[8]

McDonald's survived NATO's bombing campaigns in Belgrade, but the real test now is French. In August 1999, Jose Bové, the head of the French farmers' union, led an attack on a McDonald's restaurant under construction in Millau, a town in the foothills of the Massif Central in southern France. Bové and almost 300 farmers effectively dismantled the fast-food outlet. The location was symbolic. The area is best known as the home of Roquefort cheese, and Bové was incensed at the US tariff of 100 per cent on gourmet French foods like Roquefort cheese, recently imposed in retaliation to the European ban on hormone-reared beef imported from the US. Bové spent 20 days in gaol, and by the time of his release was a celebrity, even attending the WTO meeting in Seattle. He spoke out against unfettered free trade and uncontrolled globalization.

The company that operated McDonald's restaurants in France fought back with an advertising campaign that poked fun at Americans and promoted the line that while McDonald's was born in the US, its food was now made in France, with French supplies and French employees. How successful the campaign will be in the long run is difficult to assess. McDonald's continues to open new outlets in France, and French consumers still order Big Macs, even though they call them Le Mac. I have spoken to young children in France who believe McDonald's to be a French company. They were shocked to learn it is American. They have grown up with French McDonald's. And while the adults continue to resist – in 1993 authorities in Paris refused permission for a McDonald's to be set up under the iconic Eiffel Tower – a generation of young French people are being socialized into eating at McDonald's without seeing it as an act of submission to US cultural and culinary imperialism.

Global Finance: Round and Round the Money Flows

By the end of the nineteenth century an international economy was fully developed. The shift from an international one to a global one was underway by the end of the twentieth century. It was neither a complete nor a uniform process. Not all companies are as footloose as shoe manufacturers, and there are barriers to technology transfers between countries. Not all countries are fully globalized. Indeed, we can more faithfully picture the economic globalization of production as consisting of a series of technology districts, 'technopoles' if you like, around the world in selected countries rather than in all countries. Regional economic complexes are the fundamental unit of the global economy rather than national economies.

Consumption is far more dispersed. Capitalist commodities have found their way into more homes in more countries than at any time in human history. Fashion consciousness has replaced class consciousness in many places around the world.

There are limits to economic globalization. It has been hampered by, among other things, tariff barriers, the persistence in many sectors of an international division of labour, and continuing state regulation of labour markets. In one area, however, it has been rapid and complete. Global financial integration, which we can define as the increasing freedom of movement, transfer and tradeability of money and finance across the globe, has become the leading edge of globalization.

On the first occasions I travelled abroad from Britain (late 1960s and early '70s) I was limited as to how much money I could take out of the country. I will always remember the stamp in my first passport noting that I had taken £15 on a trip to Spain. That was the maximum limit. Back then, going to a bank in a foreign country to get money out was a exercise requiring patience and fortitude. If I visit Spain now, or indeed almost any country, I carry a small plastic card and get the local currency just as soon as I punch in the numbers at an ATM; the bill arrives at my home in US dollars. Money knows no boundaries. The finance system has moved from a national to a globally integrated system, with the consequent loss of national financial autonomy. The transcendent power of money to break national boundaries is one of the most pronounced features of globalization.

The move to global monies began with the fall of the Bretton Woods system. This system, established in 1944, was an attempt to both maintain national economic sovereignty and create an open international system of trade and investment. The system was based on fixed exchange rates and a series of national financial regulations. The US dollar was the convertible medium of currency with a fixed relationship to the price of gold, $35 an ounce. The system seemed to guarantee both national sovereignty and international economic cooperation. The system collapsed in the early 1970s. The costly Vietnam War mean that the US was racking up huge trade deficits and suffering rapid inflation. International confidence was ebbing. The ability to end the War, never mind win it, forced a reassessment of US power and dependence. The Vietnam War undermined the fiscal strength of the country and eroded international confidence. In 1971 President Nixon announced that the dollar was no longer freely convertible to gold. The devaluation of the dollar signalled the end of fixed exchange rates. When fixed exchange rates disappeared and every domestic currency was convertible into every other, the value of currencies was set by worldwide demand and supply. The global market rather than national politicians now set exchange rates. A fundamental element of national economic sovereignty, the ability to set the exchange rate of a currency, had been taken out of the hands of politicians and put into those of currency speculators. In this context, IMF surveillance took on more power, since it became important to know the underlying worth of a country's currency and hence the validity of prevailing exchange rate. The Bretton Woods system was a system of stability that promised both international economy and national sovereignty. Post Bretton Woods, the volatile system of floating exchange rates allowed global financial integration at the cost of national sovereignty.

The demise of fixed exchange rates undermined national financial regulations and thus allowed easier capital flows across national borders. There were two other factors that lubricated the flow. The first was Eurocurrencies. These were first created in the 1950s and 1960s when the USSR and some East European countries deposited their US dollars in European banks to avoid them being taken by the US government. Then multinationals began to deposit their foreign currency earnings in the form of Eurocurrencies in order to avoid tax and regulations in their home countries. A pool of 'denationalized' money was created. Corporations, and even national governments, used the Euro market to borrow and to raise foreign currency. A denationalized money had been created.

Second, the oil price hike imposed by OPEC in 1973, from $2.48 a barrel to $11.65 a barrel, meant a huge transfer of funds from oil-importing countries to oil-exporting countries. The current account balance of OPEC countries increased from $1.5 billion in 1972 to $7 billion in 1977. The oil exporters became the *nouveaux riches* of the global economy. Some of them used it to undertake ambitious programmes. The Shah of Iran began a large military build-up and an extensive modernization programme. The programme was unpopular with many religious leaders, who eventually fused anti-Shah feelings with religious fundamentalism into a movement that eventually swept away the Shah and his secular government. But even the most ambitious schemes could not soak up all the new-found money. The insatiable demand for oil meant that the revenues kept pouring in. Many of the oil exporters invested in international money markets. A great pool of liquid money was created. Some of it was lent to cash-poor, newly industrializing countries and the poorer oil-importing countries who were facing a cash shortfall. The current account balance of poor, non-oil-exporting countries fell from minus $5 billion in 1972 to minus $36 billion. By 1979 international banks had lent $150 billion to poor, oil-importing countries.

The fall of fixed exchange rates and the growth of Eurocurrencies and petrodollars together created a more liquid financial system. Money became less a national currency and more an international medium of exchange. An institutional infrastructure of international banks and global markets was created.

A variety of global financial flows can be identified. One of the most obvious is foreign direct investment (FDI), which is the investment of corporations in other countries. For example, Korean shoe manufacturers now invest money in factories in China, Indonesia, Nicaragua and

Vietnam. These flows have tripled from $192 billion in 1988 to $610 billion in 1998. The largest chunk of FDI, almost two-thirds, takes place between rich countries: US companies investing in British factories, French banks taking over small US banks. Rich countries are the main recipients and the main sources of FDI. Only one quarter of all FDI goes to developing countries; it is unevenly spread. China, Korea and Singapore account for half of this, with China taking the largest share – almost one-third – of all FDI to developing countries. These private-sector flows, now the largest form of capital inflow to developing countries, dwarf the $15 billion poverty reduction investment programme of the World Bank in 2000. While FDI is a mixed bag, sometimes bringing the poor working conditions found in Nike factories in Korea and Indonesia, and environmental degradation, the real tragedy for poor countries is the lack of FDI. The lion's share of FDI is going to only a few developing countries. In much of sub-Saharan Africa, FDI is minimal. The World Bank poverty reduction programme offsets some, but the lack of capital investment is hindering development, growth and increased living standards.

Not receiving foreign investment is worst. The poorest countries in the world are getting none. They are starved of funds, just as their peoples are starved of food. It is not globalization that is the problem, it is the exclusion from the benefits of globalization: access to global markets, increased living standards and the democratization that often accompanies economic growth in market economies. They are also excluded from the rising tide of economic growth. The share of world trade held by the poorest countries was only 0.4 per cent in 2000, and that was 50 per cent less than it was in 1980. Despite the rising absolute increase in world trade, this diminishing proportion is evidence of exclusion from the global economy.

There are also capital market flows that involve international transactions in securities, bonds, notes, derivatives and currencies. By the mid-1990s these totalled almost $600 billion. Savers have diversified their portfolios to include foreign assets in the form of bonds, equities and loans, and lenders have turned to foreign as well as domestic sources for funds. It is possible to speak of international bonds, international equities and international money markets.

Let us briefly consider the international money markets in which currencies are traded. Foreign exchange markets are concentrated in London, Tokyo and New York, with a second tier in Hong Kong, Frankfurt, Zurich and Paris. The total foreign exchange turnover increased from $17.5 trillion in 1979 to $297.5 trillion in 1995. Currencies are traded, bought and sold, but also speculated, as investors take positions, betting on the future exchange rate of one or more currencies. Unlike domestic stock markets, the foreign exchange market is a 24-hour one. Between them, London, New York and Tokyo provide a 24-hour coverage. The market is turbulent, speculative and sensitive. A small run against a currency in Tokyo can pick up steam in London, generate further speed in New York and become a full flight when the market opens again in Tokyo. Runs against a currency can lead to a marked devaluation and consequent economic crisis. Devaluations effected the Mexican *peso* in 1994 and the Russian *rouble* in 1998. In both cases the currencies had to be bailed out by loans from other governments and the IMF. One of the most dramatic cases was the Asian crisis of 1997. It began with a run against the Thai currency but extended to many East Asian countries. The South Korean *won*, for example, fell from around 800 *won* to the dollar on 10 January 1997 to almost 2000 *won* to the dollar two days later. In order to shore up its foreign currency reserves and pay back short-term loans, the Korean government entered into agreement with the IMF in November 1997. In return for a $56 billion loan package, the Korean government was forced to cut public spending, increase excise and other indirect taxes, relax import limitations, hold inflation below 5 per cent, allow international investors to own 50 per cent or more of Korean companies and allow foreign banks access to the domestic market. Korea was 'opened' for foreign investment and control. Unemployment rose, layoffs occurred, and even those in employment saw their purchasing power fall by almost 50 per cent.

We can look at the Korean situation in a number of ways. In one way it shows the power of the foreign-exchange markets to undermine domestic policies. The national economy of South Korea was undermined by speculative currency trading that forced the government to implement deflationary and reform measures. This story is one of globalization sweeping away national sovereignty. But there is another narrative. In this alternative tale, the problems for Korea stem from domestic issues of failing corporations, large loans made more on the basis of friendship and connection than sound financial criteria, and a banking system riven with cronyism, inefficiency and lack of transparency. The currency crisis merely reinforced the domestic bungles. South Korea, which had been happy to be involved in the global trading system as long as it was prospering from cheap exports sent to foreign markets, now found itself held accountable by the global system. There are elements of truth in both stories. The first one has more currency in South Korea.

One of the fastest growing areas of the global financial system is the growth of derivatives. They take three forms: futures, options and swaps. Futures trading is an agreement to trade a commodity (pork bellies, copper, wheat) or even a currency at an agreed future date for an agreed price. Initially devised to provide stability and guaranteed prices for commodity dealers, it has expanded to become a major source of speculative activity. Futures agreements are bought and sold as dealers try to buy the future prices for less than the final price. Options are when an agreement is struck so that the holder has the right to buy an agreed quantity of the commodity/currency at an agreed price on a certain date. Swaps are, as the name implies, agreements to swap payments in two separate transactions: I will swap my pork bellies futures for your copper futures.

Derivatives trading has grown enormously from around $600 billion in 1986 to $10 trillion today. And it is with derivatives currency trading that we return to the story of the fall of Barings in 1995.

Barings was a merchant bank with a long history. John Baring emigrated from Bremen in Germany to Exeter in England and, in 1717, started a wool business. His son founded the family banking firm in London in 1763. It prospered, and the Barings became earls, knights, viceroys and barons as they transformed raw capital into cultural capital, new money into old respectability. The firm was enmeshed in imperial ventures. The company helped finance the British war effort against Napoleon, organized loans in South America and was the principal agent in the financing of US foreign trade and the sale of US bonds. In 1890 the government of Argentina defaulted on a loan and Barings was left with a £21 million liability. It was bailed out by the Bank of England. Barings subsequently had a history of conservatism. By the 1990s it was no longer a dominant player, but, like every other financial institution, was involved in global trading. It was one of the first foreign institutions to get a place at the Tokyo Stock Exchange. Barings wanted to take part in the Asian economic miracle. In 1984 it bought an Asian stockbroking business that was the basis for Barings Securities, which made money on the then bullish Tokyo stock market. The bubble economy burst in the early 1990s and Barings Securities lost $20 million in 1992. In the same year Nick Leeson was sent out as head of settlements, becoming head of trading with a speciality in futures trading.

The losses run up by Leeson in 1995 resulted from trading on the Singapore, Osaka and Tokyo exchanges. Leeson had taken futures on the assumption that the Nikkei was not going to fall. It did. It fell 1000 points (from 19,000) on 23 January 1995. Downwards it went, and Leeson doubled the bet. Bankers asked for more money to cover the position. Barings had only $316 million in reserves and the losses were $1.4 billion. This time the Bank of England refused to bail them out. Other banks refused to cover for Barings because the losses were so large and there was no cap to the liability. Barings declared bankruptcy in February 1995.

The bankruptcy sent a shock around the financial system. Japan's

Nikkei fell 3.8 per cent. The key indexes in Philippines and Taiwan fell 4 per cent and 3 per cent respectively. The British pound faltered in international trading and the shares of British banks and financial companies associated with Barings fell around 6 per cent. The Bank of England made plans for providing liquidity to the British banking system if a crisis developed. It never did.

The term 'rogue trader' was used a lot in the newspaper coverage. Barings, Singapore's and London's financial communities, indeed the global financial community, held on to the rogue trader theory. Like the lone gunman theory, this narrative shifts attention away from structural issues to wayward individuals. However, Leeson needed large amounts of funds to even be involved in futures trading, which meant that Barings head office had channeled funds to Singapore. Barings gave Leeson such a free hand because he was making money by speculating. Successful traders only become rogue traders when they lose money. It became clear in later investigations that the Barings head office had no idea of the intricacies of derivatives trading. It is a complex and arcane field. Its mysteries allow those on the inside to operate without outside control or knowledge.

Leeson was not the only 'rogue trader'. In 1996 Sumitomo Corporation announced that its chief copper trader, Yasuo Hamanaka, lost almost $2 billion over a decade of copper trading. The former oil-trading chief of Metallgesellschaft of Germany lost more than $1 billion. In 1994 the very wealthy Orange County in southern California declared bankruptcy after its chief officer, Robert Citron, lost $1.7 billion on investments in derivatives, in particular, futures on the direction of interest rates. Human stupidity and venality is a constant; the forms they take vary according to circumstance. A global financial system and the risky areas of futures raises the opportunities for both.

All morality plays, and the Barings story was often represented as a morality story of greed and ambition followed by suffering and redemption, end with the consequences. For our ethical edification, where are they now?

Barings: The bank declared bankruptcy in 1995 and was purchased by a Dutch banking and insurance company, ING, thus ending the independent existence of one of the world's oldest and most respected merchant banks.

Nick Leeson: On 25 February 1995 Leeson fled Singapore. He was arrested when he landed in Germany and was put into gaol in Frankfurt. He returned to Singapore in November and was charged with 11 counts of forgery and fraud. Singapore was keen to prosecute Leeson in order to maintain its position as a financial hub in the global economy. It was alleged, and later proved, that Leeson had forged documents, pretending he was acting on behalf of clients, and misled the company into thinking he had enough reserves to cover speculative futures trading. He was gaoled for seven years for fraud. He was released in July 1999 because he was suffering from bowel cancer. He returned to Britain and is currently studying psychology at Middlesex University.

The global financial system: Despite the fears, there was no financial meltdown in the wake of the Barings collapse. Senior bankers and respected politicians were seriously worried that a relatively small merchant bank could cause such havoc. It reveals an underlying nervousness that the global financial system, and especially the derivatives market, which now is a $14 trillion market, is a crisis waiting to happen. So-called rogue traders simply highlight the uncertainty, the opportunity for mayhem, the unlimited liability, the speculative nature of it all. The Chancellor of the British Exchequer made a statement to the House of Commons on 27 February 1995. He repeated the rogue trader theory: 'This failure is of course a blow to the City of London. But it appears to be a specific incident unique to Barings centred on one rogue trader in Singapore.' In the same speech he also remarked on the 'need to ensure effective regulation of international dealings in derivatives'. Currently, there is no effective regulation.

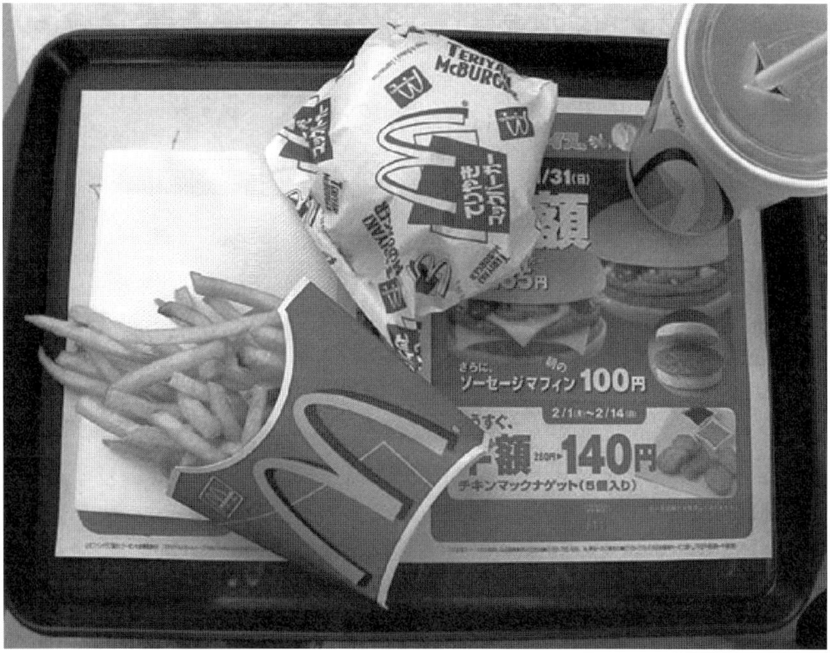
さらに、
朝の
ソーセージマフィン 100円
140円
チキンマックナゲット(5個入り)

CHAPTER FIVE

Global Cultures

India. At 9 pm, Monday to Thursday throughout the summer and autumn months of 2000, almost 100 million people watched *Kaun Banega Crorepati*. In the US, at the equivalent time slot, TV viewers also tuned in to watch *Who Wants to be a Millionaire?* Both shows were wildly popular. Different country, but the same show, created by the British production company Celador and sold to over 30 countries, including Argentina, Finland, Israel and Japan. The format is identical. The same set design, the same patter and catch-lines – *Are you sure? Is that your final answer?* The formula is contained in a production manual of over 300 pages, and British technicians train the local crews. There are differences. The pitchman in the US is Regis Philbin, one of those affable personalities best known for being ... well, an affable personality. In India the veteran film actor Amitabh Bachchan is the question-master. The questions are also tailored to national audiences. The show is crafted from a basic model to suit specific national markets. Different countries, same TV programme. The show has become globalized. Different programmes, same basic model. The show has become glocalized.

The world has been culturally globalized by continuous, increasing and deepening flows of not only TV shows but also goods, people, capital, ideas and information across national boundaries. A number of forces have contributed to the facilitation of these flows, including the emergence of international organizations, global spectacles and competitions, advances in technologies and global entertainment industries.

The debates on cultural globalization have polarized into whether the recent surge of cultural flows and global consciousness have increased or decreased sameness between people and places around the world. The cultural homogenization account points to the formation of a global consumer culture in the era of late capitalism. The assertion goes something like this: the world is becoming more alike as more of it watches formulaic TV shows and Disney movies and consumes Coca-Cola and Big Macs. For some, this globalization is a form of American cultural imperialism whereby US products, goods and values are diffused, creating similarity where previously there was difference. It is a compelling image that captures some, if not all, of the complexity. The fact that people across the globe are watching CNN and MTV, that McDonald's is opening outlets everywhere, and that many Hollywood films dominate the world film market are taken as indisputable evidences of the homogenization and Americanization of the world. The homogenization thesis assumes the same things are consumed in the same ways.

An alternative thesis is that, while particular TV programmes, sports spectacles, network news, advertisements and films may rapidly encircle the globe, this does not mean that the responses of those viewing and listening will be uniform. Goods, ideas and symbols may be diffused globally, but they are consumed within national and local cultures. Eating a Big Mac does not make one an apologist for US foreign policy. Ideas, symbols and goods that circulate around the world are consumed in national contexts and in local circumstances. Smoking, in large parts of the US, is seen as an uncivil act, while in China to smoke is to be cool and hip. Similar goods mean different things in different places. There are enough variances to suggest that there is little prospect of a unified global culture; there is at present a variety of active global cultures.

Specific cultural backgrounds are not just empty containers for the receipt of global messages, they are critical to how messages are received and consumed. People in the contemporary world have become increasingly familiar with the presence of other cultures, rather than experiencing a single cultural orbit.

Global flows of culture are continually shaping and reshaping the world. Arjun Appadurai identifies five sites or realms in which these flows can be identified: ethnoscapes, technoscapes, financescapes, mediascapes and ideoscapes. These realms signify, respectively, the changes in the 'landscapes of persons', technologies, finances or capital flows, the media, and the political configurations of ideas such as freedom, welfare rights, sovereignty, representation and democracy. Migration and media introduce and mobilize elements of culture so that they circulate globally and become re-expressed through local contexts.

Locality itself is a historical product. The processes that shape localities are not one-way interactions, they are dynamic and multifaceted, so that hybrids of the 'newly arrived' and the 'previously there' are constantly reconfigured and remobilized through global flows. Locality is produced through cultural practices. Appadurai gives the example of cricket in India, formerly 'an instrument for socializing black and brown men into the public etiquette of empire, it is now an instrument for mobilizing national sentiment in the service of transnational spectacles and commoditization'.[9] Thus the sport that is firmly embedded in India's colonial past is now a symbol of its independent national pride.

Culture is not just passive audiences watching imported TV programmes or eating fast food from global chains. Culture is an active process: one definition of culture is the tending, the husbanding of resources – the same root as *cultivation*. A culture is not just the consumption of things; it is the production of a world view, an aesthetic sensibility, the active creation of a history and geography, the working out of a place in the world. Cultural expression is as much a fact as cultural consumption. Culture is associated with place in complex ways; it is more than just a passive receptor, the end-point on the pathway of a global commodified culture. Culture involves the active use of these global flows into local, national and group-specific views of the world. To be sure, more people around the world can draw on a similar range of flows, but there is still a wide variety of cultural formations. In fact, cultural globalization has led to a more explicit concern with more local cultures as certain groups seek to redefine or re-establish their place in the world.

When we speak about culture in the current debate on globalization there is a tendency to counterpoise a local, unchanging culture with a new, bland Americanized culture. But cultures are not unchanging, static remnants of bygone ages. Cultures are active processes of assimilation and hybridization. All cultures are mixtures of the global and local, the past and present. Cultures are not pure states, they are active processes of hybridization. Cultures appropriate and mimic other cultures. They always have. To believe that local cultures are being swamped by global commodity culture is to ignore the mixing already embodied in local cultures.

We can replace the popular image of local cultures under assault from a global culture with a more complex picture of local cultures being generated and recreated in response to globalization. The sense of a pervasive globalization has not so much overwhelmed local cultures as helped create them. The search for authenticity, for pure local cultures (which are in fact mixtures) has helped in the creation of world music, ethnic cuisine and indigenous culture. Religious fundamentalism is less a return to a pure theocratic ideology and more the self-conscious recreation of religious beliefs in the face of secularization and globalization. Cultural authenticity is less an excavation of the pure and more a contemporary representation of the contrived.

There is no simple division between a local and a global culture. Take clothes. Around the world there is an increasing uniformity of clothes, especially by age group. Young people everywhere have a similarity about them. But the same can also be said about the transnational business class or creative intellectuals. Each group has been globalized in one sense in terms of their clothing; so students around the world are looking alike, just as business executives have a similar look to them. But there is also a return to ethnic looks. In Australia the cult of the Bush has its expression in city dwellers, who wear the suits of the transnational business class during the week but switch to country style boots and hats for the weekend. In Japan many couples go through two marriage ceremonies, one in Western dress, the other in traditional costume. When I got married to my American wife in Palo Alto, California, the Scottish kilts I and my brother wore were hired from a company in New Hampshire. A return to the local. But kilts themselves are largely the product of the imagination of Prince Albert, the German-born husband of Queen Victoria, who in the nineteenth century helped foster the idea of a traditional Scotland full of kilts, which in reality had never existed. The kilt is an example of a 'national' culture that was not so much pure as imagined. Wearing a kilt at a wedding in the US was not an expression of an authentic, ancient culture, but a hybridized culture recreated in order to stress authenticity and distinctiveness in the face of the globalization of clothing styles.

A fuller understanding of cultural globalization has to move beyond the sameness/difference dichotomy to a fuller sense of the enduring tension between difference and sameness. The co-presence of homogenizing and heterogenizing trends might be a better phrase to describe the processes of cultural globalization, rather than a binary classification of globalizing/non-globalizing. We can unravel some of this complexity further by looking in detail at culture's commodification, its Americanization and its de-territorialization.

Capitalize Culture

In his novel *Babbitt* (1922), Sinclair Lewis has one of his characters, a small-town businessman, report that

> Culture has become as necessary an adornment for a city today as pavements or bank-clearances. It's Culture, in theaters and art galleries and so on, that brings thousands of visitors to New York every year and, to be frank, for all our splendid attainments we haven't got the Culture of a New York or Chicago or Boston – or at least we don't get the credit for it. The thing to do then, as a live bunch of go-getters is to capitalize Culture; to go right out and grab it.

Cultural globalization has been reinforced by the capitalization of culture. Sports, music, art, cinema, dance have all been commodified. Take soccer. Soccer started off as a working-class game in Britain. It developed in the nineteenth century in the industrial heartlands. Big cities like Glasgow, Liverpool, Manchester, Newcastle upon Tyne all boasted local soccer teams. The Football Association was established in 1867 and began the national competition, the FA Cup, in 1871. In the course of the twentieth century, teams became ever more professional – paying players and charging onlookers. A recreation was becoming a sport, and that sport was becoming a business. In the second half of the twentieth century the game gradually became more international. The World Cup – the competition between national teams held every four years – grew in size and prestige, becoming the showpiece of the game. At club level in Europe and South America, international competitions became as much highlights of the season as national competitions. And by the end of the twentieth century, the clubs at the elite level throughout Europe were drawing in players from around the world. The players were international, and so was the coverage, becoming a staple in many media markets. And the result: soccer is the world's most popular game, and you can find Manchester United fans all over the world following their team, which, at the time of writing, is managed by a Scotsman and has a French goalkeeper.

Not every sport can go global. Despite their best intentions, not all the sports in the US have achieved global penetration. The National Hockey League, for example, has yet to achieve the international acceptability of the National Football Association and National Basketball Association. However, on a visit to Finland in 1996, I discovered that most of the sports coverage during one week of an overcast October was of NHL fixtures, especially those in which Finnish players were prominent. No US game has achieved the global dominance of soccer. While Major League Baseball is big in parts of Central and South America, it has yet to find popular acceptance in Europe.

The commodification of culture is embodied in the growth and power of the media industry. And just as in other industries, we can identify large multinational corporations. The largest media corporation is Time Warner, which, in 2000, had sales of $28 billion. Time Warner is a giant company that incorporates Time Life Books; cable TV shows, such as HBO and CNN, with local variants around the world; magazines such as *Time*, *Sports Illustrated* and *People*; over 50 recording labels, including Reprise, Electra, Maverick, Giant and Warner Music; theme parks; retail outlets, including almost 200 Warner Bros Studio Stores in over 30 countries; entertainment networks, such as TBS, TNTV and the Cartoon Network; three film production companies; and multiplex movie theatres in over 12 countries. Time Warner has interests in Asia, Europe and South and North America. Around the world Warner films, with film scores from Warner recording artists, are shown in Warner cinemas and reviewed in Warner magazines with marketing spin-offs in Warner Bros stores.

The commodification of culture does lead to a certain similarity in the cultural mix available to audiences around the world. But the more astute companies tailor their cultural products for specific audiences. Hybridity is a feature of globalized commodified culture. Multinational corporations such as McDonald's, Guinness and Coca-Cola are adopting practices of hybridization to make their global staples local favourites. Guinness hires locals in its factory in Accra, Ghana, and McDonald's includes vegetarian menu items in India. One of the guiding directives of presentation to these commercial giants is that successful brands are personal, an integral part of people's lives. Emotional connections are forged by engaging with local cultures and hybridizing global brands.

The term global localization was first coined by Akio Morita, the legendary head of Sony. It was a business strategy conceived in order to establish worldwide operations that were attuned to local markets and conditions. It was reinforced by rising incomes around the world. As per capita income increases, consumers want good quality products regardless of where they are made. Those consumers with annual incomes above $26,000 go global. Indeed, going global is a sign of affluence and sophistication. Global consumers and global companies are creating a globalized consumer industry, albeit tailored to specific national markets and local conditions.

A cultural economy can be identified across a variety of scales. At the global level we can see the emergence of consumers and companies. At the more local level there is a connection between cultural and economic globalization. Economic globalization puts pressure on cities to develop their specific cultures in ways that will attract business and investment, and convince their own residents and entrepreneurs to remain. Cosmopolitan diversity and cultural sophistication have become as essential ingredients of successful global cities as are international airports and luxury hotels. The commodification of culture is closely connected to the globalization of the economy.

The Americanization of Culture?

The sameness of cultural globalization is a place-specific sameness. It overwhelmingly emanates from the US. There are some who see companies such as Coca-Cola, McDonald's and Disney and their associated products as the Trojan horse of American cultural imperialism. We have some images to reinforce this view. A few years after Desert Storm, a McDonald's opened in Kuwait City. On the opening day in 1994, 15,000 customers waited in a seven-mile-long queue of air-conditioned cars. First the US military liberated the city from Saddam Hussein; then McDonald's moved in.

Let me be frank. I see no such simple connection, but the image is a powerful one that many believe. My disbelief is not based on any naïve reading of US companies. They do want to dominate the world, but they want to do so in order to make money. They sell what they think people want. Is it leading to a bland set of Americanized consumers. I don't think so.

US companies, and even that term is problematic, are moving away from the simple globalizing strategies towards more glocalizing strategies. Take the Coca-Cola company. In an average year it sells soft drinks in over 200 countries around the world and makes annual profits of $2 billion. Coca-Cola sells its trademark brand around the world, and has done so for some time. The famous drink was first sold in Argentina in 1942, in Belgium in 1927 and in Italy in 1925. In recent years it has branched out from its core brands of Coke, Sprite and Fanta to sell 'local' brands:

Australia	Lift
China	Smart, Tian Yu Di
India	Gold Spot, Limca, Maaza, Thumbs Up
Japan	Calo, Ambasa, Shpla
South Africa	Iron Brew
UK	Lilt
Sweden	Mer

Nigeria	Quatro
Brazil	Tai
Venezuela	Chinotto

Two waves of Coca-Cola globalization can be identified. The first and earliest involved marketing and selling the original drink. The second, and more recent, has involved both the sale of Coca-Cola but also the sale and marketing of 'local' brands. The Coca-Cola company's soft drinks in Brazil are often marketed as rain-forest drinks with 'forest' tastes and plant sources. The company is both globalizing and glocalizing.

'McDonald's Around the World' has widely been used to describe the dramatic globalization of American cultural products. McDonald's currently has over 28,000 restaurants in 120 countries. An enormous number of Big Macs and fries are being consumed. One per cent of the world's population eats at McDonald's. Its restaurants in Japan added the Teriyaki McBurger to the regular menu, and now some McDonald's restaurants in the US provide Teriyaki and other sauces. McDonald's has been glocalized in Japan, and the Japanese McBurgers, in part, have changed the original McDonald's in the US. The local is being influenced by the global as much as the global is being changed by the local. A similar pattern can be found in the film industry. As more and more US films are sold abroad, American film-makers have to keep foreign markets in mind. In the case of Japan, for example, movies with disabled people do not do well, nor does sophisticated wordplay, for much of it is lost in translation. The bad guy *has* to lose. There has been a shift in Hollywood, at least in terms of the very expensive movies that require foreign sales, towards more action movies with similar plots. The particularities of US life are being replaced in expensive Hollywood movies by images, plots and characters that are instantly recognizable in foreign markets. Hollywood, like McDonald's when it goes global, is affected by the local.

There is nothing specifically American about Coca-Cola or

McDonald's. However, with Disney, a more complex argument needs to be made because Disney sells ideas, dreams and fantasies rather than sugared drinks or burgers. Coca-Cola and McDonald's are also in the business of fantasy – food and drink is a world of fantasy – but not so explicitly as film companies are.

Disney is the second largest cultural corporation after Time Warner. Under its banner it sells books, films and music; it controls radio and TV networks, themes parks and resorts. In 1997 it had sales of $24 billion. Its chairman, Michael Eisner, regularly makes $10 million per year, and in one stock option move Disney made almost $600 million. What Disney creates are movies and TV programmes. And they have to be global in scope to make money. It is almost impossible for an expensive movie to make profits without an overseas market. However, Hollywood movies tend to draw on US themes to provide the narrative drive and meaning. In that sense Disneyfication is Americanization. But what exactly is this America that is being represented? It is an America that has to appeal to a heterogeneous experience even within the US. In order for things to sell well even within the US, they have to be smoothed out so that they succeed throughout the country. Much of the warp and weft of life in specific parts of the US is filtered through the need to reach a more general national market. A case can be made that American culture has been so successful in achieving global penetration because it has already been partly globalized just in order to reach a wide US audience. The US is so diverse and heterogeneous that cultural products have to be smoothed out in order to succeed, and that in itself primes them for global dispersal.

We can point to other countries that have been successful in achieving global cultural niches. The nostalgia that pervades cultural life in the UK has been embodied in the ability of TV and film companies to make wonderful period pieces. Numerous novels by Charles Dickens and Jane Austen have been successfully translated for the screen and achieved worldwide success. Similarly, French infatuation with food and drink has enhanced the globalization of French gastronomy and luxury food items.

The US has been most successful at popular cultural items like film, fast food and sugared drinks. But it is less an Americanization and more a successful commodification. The real success story of Disney, Coca-Cola and McDonald's is not the Americanization of the world, but its commodification. The winner is capitalism more than it is Americanism.

Culture and Place

Some have argued that there has been a de-territorialization of culture. Globalization processes, it has been said, have greatly accelerated the disconnection between original identity and traditional location.

When we think of culture we often think of distinctive songs, dances, foods – all those things that go to make up collective memories and group identities. In much of our understanding these are tied to place: Mexican food, Indian music, Italian design, Armenian dance. But international migrations, the flows of people and ideas, the commodification and transnationalization of cultural aspects, have all broken the simple connection between culture and place.

But on closer inspection, the connection between culture and place was always problematic. 'Mexican' food is a mixture of Spanish and indigenous cuisines that have evolved in different parts of the country in different ways for almost 400 years. The process of de-territorialization began long before the current round of globalization. The Spaniards and Africans who arrived in the New World combined with indigenous peoples to create a New World cuisine that was creolized and hybridized right from the beginning. There is no unchanging New World cuisine. Mexican food is itself a modifying hybrid.

The relation of identity and location has always been problematic. Massive emigration from Scotland (I draw on my own experience here) means that for a long time there have been as many Scots living outside of Scotland as there are inside. But does being Scots change in meaning or experience if one doesn't live in Scotland? Yes. But is one more authentic than the other? I think not. They are similar, but different. And they are connected. Expatriate Scots have shaped 'Scots' identity as much as those who have never left Scotland.

This is by way of a providing a particular context for my contention that cultures are always in the process of de-territorialization and re-territorialization. The process has quickened and diffused more widely, but it is not a new process. Detroit has one of the largest 'Arab' populations outside of the Middle East. Melbourne is the fourth largest 'Greek' city in the world. The quotation marks indicate the ambiguous nature of these identities.

But has the intensification of global communications and international migration led to a more pronounced rise of de-territorialized signs, meanings and identities? The concept of de-territorialization helps us understand the cultural dimensions of globalization, which have been too narrowly defined by the concept of the Americanization or homogenization of the world. However, the term is not really suggestive of the resilient presence and, in many cases, the flourishing expression of heterogeneity around the world. We need another concept, re-territorialization, to describe the process by which de-territorialized cultures take roots in places far from their traditional locations and origins. The re-territorialization of a culture embraces a series of processes that range from diffusion from their origin across borders (spatial, temporal and cultural) to establishment in a new place in a new form. Re-territorialized cultures are not simply transposed, they are transformed, reflecting the assertion of locality in a globalizing world.

Globalization, it has been argued, undermines local identities. Yet an alternative case can be made that globalization has both de-territorialized and strengthened local cultures. In the nineteenth century there was a massive emmigration to the US from many European countries. Italians, Germans, Poles and Irish crosed the Atlantic in their millions. Once there, connection with home was limited, separated as they were by rudimentary communication links. Letters could take weeks. New identities were created. People from different parts of what is now Italy became Italians in the US. New identities were shaped. Irish Americans took on the mythic elements of Irish nationalism. Folk memories did not die; indeed, in many cases, they became both strengthened and frozen in time. The American Irish, unlike the Irish Irish, could scarcely remember anything other than the Great Famine.

In recent years, however, immigrants in the US have been able to maintain closer connections with their families back home. Cheaper telephone rates, email, more affordable plane journeys; all those easier communication systems of a globalized world have allowed groups to be more in touch with their home areas. They are now closer to home than immigrants have ever been simply because of globalization. (Of course, what home represents is always changing too.)

My contention is that globalization has not disrupted the connection between culture and place. That disconnection has been occuring for at least 2000 years. Cultures have been mixing and changing; places have been impacted by forces from around the world. There is no untouched culture in a purely local place. Globalization has put new wrinkles on the connection. The more recent round of globalization has done three things. In its commodification of selected cultural forms it has transformed some 'local' cultures into globalized forms. Indian restaurants outside India, for example, serve food that is never found in restaurants in India. Second, it has involved the glocalization of global brands into local and national markets. Third, it has rendered more complex the relationship between identity and place. The flows of ideas and images allow re-territorialization of cultures. Armenians in the US can more easily keep in touch with Armenians in Armenia. Contemporary realities can replace old stories locked in at the historical time of the migration. Easier flows of people and money allow more connected diasporas, and thus group identity is being shaped by outsiders as well as insiders.

Culture and place are connected, but not in simple unchanging ways. In a globalizing world the connections between place and culture are an unstable complex mode of representation.

English as a Global Language

Cultural globalization is intimately connected with the development of English as a global language. English is the hegemonic language of the contemporary world. The extensive impact of the British Empire during the colonial period, and the dominance of the American economy and its culture, science, technology and politics in the contemporary world have all led to the supremacy of English. It has become the *lingua franca* of global interaction. English is the language of international interaction. Most scientific, technological and academic information in the world is expressed in English, and over 80 per cent of all information stored in electronic retrieval systems is in English. English is the language of international entertainment, popular music, movies and advertising. By 1995, 75 countries officially recognized English as a primary or secondary language. The number of people who speak English as a first or second language has been estimated at approximately 573 million. A further 670 million may have native-like fluency in the language. Even non-speakers are exposed to the language on a daily basis through advertising, government functions or inter-personal communication. In *English as a Global Language*, David Crystal describes those with English as members of an expanding circle who have, via the dynamic processes of globalization, been exposed to the language on many informal levels. Almost 1.6 billion – over a fifth of the world's population – exhibits some reasonable competence in English.

A growing global competency in English has accelerated the rate of cultural globalization by facilitating the movement of ideas and information. The expanding use of English around the world is not, however, simply the result of diffusion outward from a dominant centre. There has been a conscious adoption. People in non-English-speaking countries have been trying to learn English in order to participate more fully in international activities.

English is required to be competitive in global markets. Many countries have adopted it as a second language and emphasize it as an important subject in their schools. One example: in the early days of the People's Republic of China (PRC), English was labelled an 'imperialist language' and its use suppressed. After China's break with the USSR, teaching Russian was abandoned and English was revived and relabelled as 'the instrument for struggles in the international stage'. In contemporary China there has been a huge increase in the use of English, fuelled by the growing number of Chinese students receiving some of their education or training in English-speaking countries, especially the US, and an increase in the demand for English-language skills among professionals and workers in the booming international trade sector. An English-language teaching industry has been developing across the country, and even those without spoken ability in English are subject to the symbols of English brand names prominent in many cities.

For individuals in many countries, English skills are an invaluable asset in the job market. Most multinational Korean companies prefer English-speaking workers because they consider them more adaptable in the global economy. English has become a form of cultural capital for both national governments seeking to produce a globally competitive workforce and for individuals eager to achieve a better position in a globalizing world.

Not only has English expanded to become the dominant worldwide medium of communicative practice, it has also undergone considerable reinvention by non-native-speaking communities, many of whom are speaking English in their own way. English as a global medium of communication is being re-territorialized within particular communities. Instead of adopting a standard form of English, non-native speakers are reshaping the language to best suit their purposes. While the introduction of English represents a de-territorialization of the language, its modification or creolization represents the ensuing re-territorialization of the language as local communities adapt the language to local needs.

English is both spoken and written, of course. Its use as a written global form of communication is particularly visible in the communities of knowledge. English has become the language of global intellectual discourse and the dominant language of intellectual communities involved in the production, reproduction and circulation of knowledge. The global epistemic community is dominated by English. For example, one very important feature of academic research is publication in journals. A sample of leading journals for the discipline of geography for the period 1981–96 reveals that the proportion of contributions from non-English-speaking countries is relatively small, ranging from 5.1 per cent to 7.4. The top journals have a distinct Anglo bias. As for the language practices of specific journals, I will give you the representative example of *Geografiska Annaler*, the journal of the Swedish Society for Anthropology and Geography.[10]

Geografiska Annaler began publication in 1919. From its inception it was intended that it should serve as an international journal. The introductory article in *Geografiska*'s first issue was written in English. It stated that the journal would be published mainly in the 'great world-languages' and in the Scandinavian languages. In 1965 it was divided into two parallel series: *Series A*, Physical Geography, and *Series B*, Human Geography. In the first issue of *Series B*, the front-page introduction explained that 'contributions are preferably published in English, French and German'. This announcement continued to appear on the front page until 1975. In

1976, however, while the *Notes for Contributors* stated that the accepted languages were English, French and German, the front-page introduction explained that published papers are mostly received in English, but that French and German may be used. In 1988 English finally secured the monopoly in *Series B* when the front-page introduction requested that papers should be written in English. The actual language practice of the published items in *Geografiska Annaler* was largely consistent with its editorial policies. Before 1965 most papers were in English, but also some in German and Swedish. No items have appeared in Swedish since 1965. Until 1988 German articles accompanied by English abstracts occasionally appeared. But since 1989 all items have been in English. An international journal from its inception, *Geografiska Annaler* has abandoned the other 'world-languages' in favour of English.

A survey of a range of geography journals reveals the increasing dominance of English in older established journals and the assumption in more recent journals that English is the only acceptable language. Geography is now dominated by one language. In a sense, publishing one's work in English has become the norm for geographers around the world. Yet the hegemony of English as the language of geographical communities appears to have been a silent revolution, neither examined nor championed.

The root definition of *geography* is 'writing about the earth'. The discipline seems skewed towards an English-writing geography from an English-speaking world. The growing dominance of English in geographical writing has advantages and disadvantages. The advantages are clear: the creation of a more global community in contrast to a series of national communities. In this sense Geography has become globalized. For those able to write in English, an international audience can be found. But those writing in languages other than English have a more restricted access to the leading journals and a wide audience.

There has been a globalization of the geographical discourse. However, it is a globalization that has been partial, uneven and redistributional. While spoken English is a much more flexible form of communication – it is legitimate to speak of global Englishes – written English, in contrast, is more rule-bound, programmatic and slow-changing. While we can think of a re-territorialization of spoken English, a re-territorialization of written English is less apparent. Written English in many knowledge-based communities, including Geography, has swept up other languages in a process of linguistic homogenization.

We lose something if we only use one language to describe the world. Languages are not just reflectors of the external world, they embody it. How we describe the world is crucially dependent on where we are and how we speak and write. The creation of a monolingual Geography raises issues about what we are losing in terms of the range and subtlety of languages used to describe the world. Daniel Nettle and Suzanne Romaine have drawn attention to the extinction of language. In their book *Vanishing Voices* (2000), they estimate that at least half the world's languages will disappear in the course of the twenty-first century. The dominance of English, as well as Mandarin and Chinese, have vanquished other languages. We are losing linguistic diversity.

There is a broader issue. In a world dominated by fewer languages we gain global communication but lose diversity, linguistic subtlety and something that is almost impossible to resuscitate: linguistic variety, like ecological diversity, may be a sign of health and vitality.

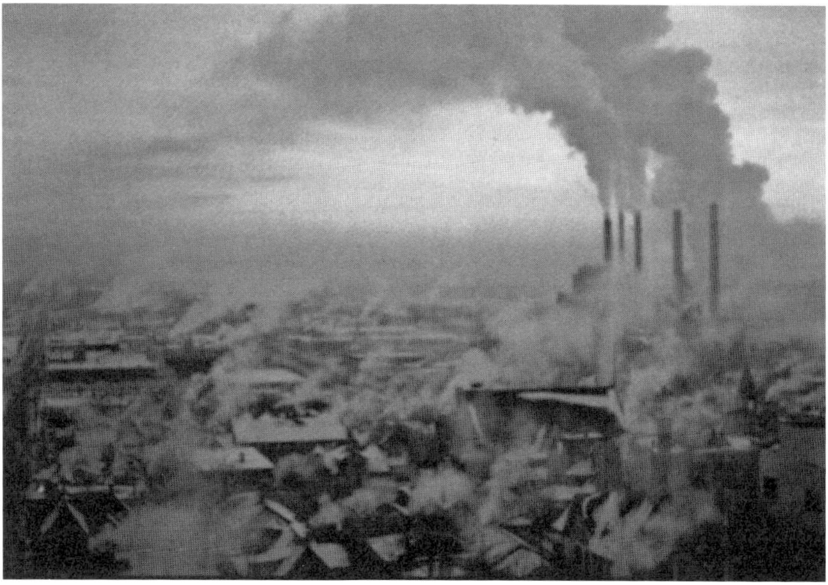

CHAPTER SIX

Border Spaces

In previous chapters we have looked at the political, economic and cultural dimensions of globalization. These are central areas of concern, but they are not the whole story. There are some interesting questions concerning the liminal areas that lie between politics and economics, culture and economics, politics and culture. Some of the more interesting aspects of globalization are to be discovered in these borderlands.

Follow the Money: Politics and Economics

In the movie *All The President's Men*, which tells the story of the Woodward and Bernstein investigation that uncovered Watergate and led to Nixon's fall, there is a scene where one of the reporters meets the secretive and anonymous source of revealing information, Deep Throat. In the dimly lit parking garage, Deep Throat tells Woodward, played by Robert Redford: *Follow the money*. To understand things, the mysterious informant repeats, you must *follow the money*. To understand much of contemporary politics it is vital to follow the money.

There has always been a connection between economics and politics. In a globalizing world the connections take on new and traditional forms. I will consider three: an economic geopolitics, an entrepreneurial state and a depoliticized economics.

The third wave of globalization began with the fall of Communism in 1989. The fall signified the end of a bipolar world divided by ideology, although there is still a rift between the rich and poor world, and the end of a geopolitics that paid little attention to domestic economic issues. During the Cold War both sides had geopolitical strategies that involved heavy arms expenditures and military budgets high enough to sustain global reach. Friendly governments were supported and sustained, crumbling elites were propped up, and direct intervention took place in Afghanistan and Vietnam, Hungary and the Dominican Republic, Czechoslovakia and Grenada. It was possible to identify a geopolitics that seemed to have less to do with national economic interest and more to do with national prestige and geopolitical considerations. The economics was clearly second to many of these considerations. What, after all, was the economic benefit of Vietnam to the US? The domino theory seems too far-fetched to justify such high costs. Geopolitics, the strategy of move and counter-move across the surface of the world, seemed to occur despite, rather than because of, national economic interests. To be sure, US power was connected to economic interests, the marines could also always be called in to stop popular revolts in banana republics, but geopolitical strategy took on a life of its own, above and beyond clearly defined national economic interests. Geopolitics was often pursued at the expense of economic efficiency and national economic health. In both the US and the USSR, resources were allocated to the military–industrial complex for weapons of mass destruction, large armies and expensive overseas presences. While Japan and West Germany were running up huge surpluses and devoting all their attention to becoming important economic powers, both the US and USSR were locked into an expensive embrace that hindered, rather than helped, their economic interests. The USSR was eventually bankrupted by the Cold War, while the US remained solvent. The real economic success stories during the Cold War were Japan and West Germany, which benefited from US military presence but paid little of the cost. It is always cheaper to be under someone else's umbrella. The US only began fully to reach its economic growth potential in the 1990s after the Cold War had ended.

The Cold War's cessation meant that a geopolitics separate from economic interests was no longer necessary, while growing economic globalization meant that it was no longer tenable. The shift in the US was amply demonstrated in the 1992 Presidential elections. On one side was an old Cold Warrior, George Bush, Vice-President under Reagan and a former head of the CIA. Bush's whole political life had been shaped by the Cold War, and its recent ending during his Presidency had taken him somewhat by surprise. On the other side was the young Governor of Arkansas, Bill Clinton, whose mantra was *It's the economy, stupid!* Clinton won for many reasons, and Bush lost for many too, but one of the most important was the feeling held by many voting Americans that national economic issues were paramount. The end of the Cold War and a recent recession had made it clear to many people that they needed a President focused on national economic issues rather than on international affairs.

The Clinton Presidency will be known for many things. In the longer term we will see it as an important transition in US foreign policy from a geopolitics to an econopolitics in which national economic interests were paramount, not secondary. The Clinton Doctrine was *foreign policy is domestic policy*. As one commentator noted, 'Clinton rearranged the traditional priorities, raising economic issues to the same level of importance as strategic affairs'.[11] It was not only that domestic economic issues received the lion's share of the President's attention. Even foreign policy was affected by this paradigmatic shift.

Clinton was not an isolationist. He used US economic power to preserve financial stability in Latin America and Asia, he pushed through NAFTA, helped engineer China's membership of the WTO and continually saw foreign policy as domestic policy writ large. The emphasis was on using US power and prestige primarily to serve US national economic interests: reducing tariffs, freeing-up markets, getting agreed-on rules for foreign investments on property rights. Not as sexy as fighting a war, and without the Kennedy-style rhetoric of 'We shall pay any price, bear any burden, meet any hardship, support any friend, oppose any foe . . .'. But the Clinton Doctrine fitted well with the Powell Doctrine, shaped essentially by the quagmire that was Vietnam, of using US forces overseas only if there was an overwhelming strategic advantage, obvious national interests at stake and a clear exit strategy. The doctrines did not halt US involvement in Bosnia, Haiti, Kosovo, Somalia or the NATO bombing of Belgrade, but they did put self-imposed limits on US foreign involvement. And even these interventions were justified in terms of humanitarian objectives after disturbing images of genocide had appeared on American TV.

Clinton was more of a globalist than an internationalist. He was concerned more with the US position in the world rather than seeing the US as the world's policeman. Under his watch, the US became more concerned with strategic global economic positioning and how to fuse domestic and foreign policies to aid the improvement of the US global economic position. Domestic economic policy influenced foreign policy by limiting military interventions, reassessing what were considered national interests and shaping a econopolitics rather than a geopolitics.

Economic globalization has also reinforced a move towards an entrepreneurial state. In the last twenty years there has been a pronounced shift towards leaner, tighter public services. The Keynsian revolution that held sway from *c.* 1945 to the mid-1970s involved a great increase in the size of the state. Public services like education, health, social security, housing and welfare all expanded. The emphasis was on redistributing wealth and opportunity. There were also state-run enterprises. The size of this sector varied in different countries. In Britain, for example, organized labour had succeeded in taking the commanding heights of the economy, including railways, steel and coalmining, into public ownership. Margaret Thatcher's election in 1979, Reagan's presidency (1980–88) and the intellectual resuscitation of the ideas of Frederick Hayek and Milton Friedman all marked a major shift in government involvement and the end of Keynsianism. The welfare state was reduced in size and importance, and with it the notion of the primary function of government as the redistributor of wealth and opportunity. In its place was the idea of government as promoter of market opportunity and economic efficiency. The welfare state was delegitimized, and the most important role of the state was as an aid to private markets. The state was not only aiding markets, it was becoming directly involved in markets. The entrepreneurial state was given form. Governments became concerned with economic efficiency and the marketization of service provision and delivery. Government departments began to look for ways to cut costs and make money. The change was particularly pronounced at the city level. Municipal governments took part in public–private ventures, often underwriting private profits with public costs, as well as becoming directly involved in land development deals, economic promotion exercises and market-driven schemes to enhance the competitive position of their city. The definition of the good urban life revolved around jobs, markets and the private sector. Public space, civic virtues and the urban public good were all tinged with this commodification and marketization.

Economic globalization has given a renewed importance to market positioning. When Nike can make shoes in many countries, and when national currencies are speculatively traded in the open market, then national policies lose their power. The power of capital, in contrast, is strengthened in a competitive global market. It is not that the state is replaced, in some cases it is strengthened as the primary carrier of regulatory functions vital to global intermeshing; rather, the political debates within the state are restricted to a range of market-aware, capital-friendly issues. Nationalization, public subsidies, welfare spending, the socialization of production become illegitimate, impossible, unthinkable. The electorate is not replaced, but the debates hinge on what is acceptable to both domestic electorates as well as international forces. In many European countries, Left-wing parties have abandoned traditional objectives. New Labour. New Democrat. The names all signal a marked change in orientation. New names for new times.

Politics has been depoliticized of basic economic differences. The right wing has won the battle of economic ideology. That makes it all the stranger to explain the level of political partisanship now remaining. We are all capitalists now. However, while economics has been depoliticized, culture has been hyper-politicized. This is most apparent in the US, where there is little difference between Democrat and Republican in terms of basic economic policy. It was a Democratic President, Bill Clinton, that introduced sweeping welfare reform, passed NAFTA and pushed for China's entry into the WTO. Substantial differences remain over issues like abortion, flag-burning, the myth rather than the reality of 'family' values. The major political differences now centre on cultural forms rather than economic issues. And the reason: while the Right has won the economic battle, it has been less successful in the cultural realm. There has been a steady liberalization in attitudes, mores and conventions since the 1960s. This came as a shock to many commentators. The pundits in Washington, DC, were shocked that an American public did not overwhelmingly denounce Clinton for the Monica Lewinsky revelations. It was clear that the US public, much more conservative than their (especially northern) European counterparts, was not as conservative as many commentators had assumed or hoped. We are all capitalists, but we are sexually sophisticated and culturally liberal capitalists.

It's Culture, Stupid! – Culture and Economics

Clinton's 1992 presidential campaign mantra – *It's the economy, stupid!* – was used to focus attention on US domestic economic issues and away from the foreign policy successes of George Bush. However, I use it here in an ironic way to highlight the fact that the distinction between domestic and foreign is not so sharp when we consider the role of cultural economics.

Culture and economics have long been considered separate and distinct. Culture has an air of refinement beyond 'vulgar economy', to use a phrase used by Jane Austen. But culture and economics are being joined in interesting combinations in a globalizing world. There is a new culture of capitalism that involves cultural production and the marketing of culture. Two themes in particular are of some interest: selling of local cultures in a global economy, and the connection between cultural networks and transnational economic flows.

Local cultural differences do not become less significant with globalization, they become more significant. First, there has been the growth of international tourism. This is not a new industry. From pilgrimages in the medieval period, through the Grand Tours of Europe in the eighteenth century, to the beginnings of mass tourism in the late nineteenth, people have been visiting other parts of the world for recreation and self-improvement. But it is an industry that has grown dramatically. In 1950 there were approximately 25 million international tourists who spent $2 billion. By the mid-1990s the comparable figures were 560 million tourists spending almost $380 billion. Tourism is a global industry of mammoth proportions, and the economy of whole regions is crucially dependent on the vagaries of the tourist trade. There are many tourist markets, but they all rely on the selling of place. Weather, vegetation, history and geography are attributes to be packaged and sold for the foreign tourist. The particularities of place – warm weather in winter, specific cuisines and interesting histories – are used to create niche markets and separate out different destinations from a homogenizing tourist space. As more international tourist hotels in different places provide the same sort of services, it is uniqueness of place and particularity of location that is highlighted, marketed and sold. Sometimes the particularities are manufactured and recreated. The self-conscious display of 'Hawaiian' culture at hotels in Waikiki and the tartan decor of hotels in Scotland are examples of invented local culture. International tourists often reinforce and sometimes create national and local stereotypes, giving a longevity to things that would otherwise have withered. Tourists create their own reality, their own sense of place. There is also the pervasive manufacturing of place particularity. My favourite example is taken from a page I tore out from a free guidebook when I was in New Zealand in 2000, referring to Queenstown in the South Island:

> 'Kiwi Magic' is now showing at the Skyline Showscan Theatre at the top of the gondola! 'Kiwi Magic' has gone to the very limits of film and sound technology to capture the magnificent splendour and awe-inspiring beauty of the New Zealand landscape. Ultra-wide 70 mm high resolution film runs 2 times faster than normal 35 mm film, coupled with a distortion-free 6 track CD sound system that envelops the audience in a sensory cocoon of actually 'being there'.

The fact that one *is* actually there seems beside this particular point. I have also seen scores of buses leaving Sydney to take people to the Blue Mountains. They sit in the bus, travel to the Blue Mountains, but only get out to see a screen that projects a film of the Blue Mountains. They could have watched the film in their hotels. Perhaps people need the phoniness of film to reinforce the sense of being, as well as of being there.

And then there are the photographers. At every scenic tourist spot there is the photo opportunity, sometimes carefully indicated on maps and by local guides. It is not about being there, but about keeping a record of having been there; as if the experience cannot be real without the accompanying snapshot. Perhaps tourists are sensing the artificiality of it all. Their presence in the photo provides a known and trusted image in a sea of make-believe.

Most tourists come from the rich countries, almost 60 per cent from North America and Europe, although there has been a steady increase in Asian tourists. Not only are the destination sites transformed and plugged into the global economy and cultural transactions, the origin areas are too. One example from my own background. More and more people in Scotland began to take overseas holidays in the 1960s. Spain was a popular destination, and soon Benidorm and Majorca replaced Blackpool and Torquay as the holiday spots of choice. When people arrived there they experienced a café culture – alcohol, coffee and food in the same setting. This was very different from the traditional Scottish pub, which was devoted purely to the consumption of alcohol – as rapidly as possible. The returning tourists brought back their experiences and pubs in Scotland began to change: food was served as well as alcohol, coffee was available and wine bars sprouted up in the big cities. Spain was not only visited, it was taken back to Scotland.

There was also a mixing of tourist experiences. The northern Europeans (Scandinavians and Germans in particular) brought to southern European beaches their love of nude bathing. I can remember lying on a beach on a small Greek island and seeing the more conservative British and Italians soon copying the Germans. The whole beach was soon a mass of naked bodies innocently displayed in a hedonistic fleshiness.

Tourism can also reinvigorate local crafts that otherwise would have perished. 'Traditional' crafts are particularly prized, since they have a feel of uniqueness, authenticity and difference that appeals to international tourists. This is not to argue that tourism is always beneficial. However, I am not one of those cultural critics who is sniffy about international tourism. There is a certain snobbishness among intellectuals – that when they go abroad, it is travel, but when others go, it is tourism. We are all tourists now. Sometimes we wreak havoc, sometimes not; sometimes our spending helps in a small measure of global redistribution, often times not. Tourism, like globalization, is a mixture of costs and benefits, unequally shared.

It is not only international tourists who are attracted by cultural particularities. As the world becomes more homogenized, more of a smooth space of limited friction and reduced transport costs, then the particularities of place become important, especially as cultural capital. This is clearly shown in the case of city promotions. Around the world, urban centres are competing for business and conventions and investment. To be a player in the game of world cities, a number of basic attributes are necessary. Some of them are obvious: good transport links, a favourable tax regime. But culture also plays a role. A solid cultural base is both the embodiment and indication of a city's relative weight. A city without an art galley or a symphony orchestra or buildings by big-name architects lacks the necessary cultural muscle to be a serious contender in the competition for world city status. When the new Getty Center designed by the architect Richard Meier opened in Los Angeles in 1998, the Director explained that 'it will make it easier for serious people to persuade themselves they might come and live in Los Angeles'. The obvious comparison is with New York, with its magnificent art museums – the Metropolitan, the Whitney, the Frick, MoMA and many others. In cultural terms Los Angeles is, and more importantly, feels itself to be, in need of some serious cultural capital.

Popular culture is also an important indicator of a city's global position in the selling of cities. Ethnic and cultural mixing of the gentler kind, not so much Jerusalem or Belfast, as San Francisco and Sydney, is highly prized. Cultural diversity, varied cuisine, ethnic carnivals, alternative lifestyles are all part of the package of pluralism. Monocultural cities are increasingly seen as provincial. To be global means to be culturally diverse.

Sometimes the cultural capital can provide a return. There is an economics to culture as well as respectability. In 1995 the Art Institute of Chicago held a four-month exhibition of Claude Monet's paintings. It was estimated that the exhibition generated $389 millions worth of benefits to the city as well as a profit of $6 million for the Art Institute. The Gay Mardi Gras in Sydney attracts 600,000 spectators and a national TV audience, and is one of the single biggest tourist attractions. The event, a celebration of cultural diversity, also adds to the cultural capital of the city and to its credibility as a world city. The pink dollar is an important part of Sydney's cultural capital and cultural economy.

In an increasingly globalized world, certain forms of cultural capital – art galleries, signature buildings, the celebration of cultural diversity in cuisine, neighbourhood types and spectacles – all become important positive attributes of place. The global world rewards these forms of commodified cultural diversity.

An important element of globalization is international migration. And along with this movement of people there has been a re-territorialization of culture. For example, we can find Chinese 'communities' in cities around the world. These cells of the diaspora can also act as important transmission points in international trade. Ethnic areas can act as networks of international trade and commerce. In Los Angeles, members of the substantial Chinese community are actively involved in trading with China, a trade aided by shared language and kinship ties. Ethnic areas can provide an anchor point for global trade. In Orange County in southern California, there is a vigorous Vietnamese community that has trading links with Vietnam. Goods made in Vietnam are shipped to Orange County, where they are repackaged and sold to the 'Vietnamese' community in the US. Cultural and ethnic ties become an important network of global economic transactions.

Ethnic entrepreneurs come in a variety of forms. There are those who connect 'home' with the diasporas. There are also those who package and sell ethnicity. In Syracuse, upstate New York, there is an Irish bar called Coleman's. The owner is an Irish-American who uses Irish not only as a source of identity but as a source of business. The bar sells Irishness – Guinness, dishes of stew and potatoes, knick-knack souvenirs from Ireland. Around the world there are many ethnic entrepreneurs who are selling difference and ethnic 'authenticity'. In the global world ethnicity, like so many other things, is commodified.

Politics and Culture: Cultural Differences, Political Divides

There has been a depoliticization of economics. Since the fall of the Soviet Union, capitalism has been triumphant around the world. We are all capitalists now. That remark is a bit simplistic, to be sure, and there are still substantial political differences between and within national states regarding the role of government, but, by and large, that bald statement holds good. Economic differences no longer have the polarizing effect they once had when there was a serious contender to capitalism. We are arguing now about how to run a capitalist economy efficiently and fairly, not how to overthrow it. The few remaining Marxists are either in the Andean mountains or are tenured professors at universities.

Politics has not withered away. There has been a more pronounced politicization of culture. A globalizing world reconnects culture and politics. The connection was never broken, but globalization highlights and reinforces the link.

Although I have spent some time in this book trying to persuade you that globalization promotes cultural difference as much as it does sameness (and the argument is surely not sophisticated enough for academic critics), it is not believed by many popular commentators. There is a genuine fear that globalization is eroding cultural identity. Whether it be seen in the wave of Hollywood movies, the opening of yet another McDonald's or the power of the WTO, the World Bank and the IMF, there is a sense felt by many people that there is something out there that is undermining traditional culture. And there is. It is not so much a vague cultural globalization as a definite specific commodification. The market economy now penetrates our private fears and dreams: we are no longer simply buying goods and services, we are buying identities and dreams. Just at the moment that capitalism emerged as triumphant, it shattered: both market segmentation and niche marketing are breaking us down into different consumption communities. The postmodern resistance to meta-narratives is exactly replicated in a capitalist market that now meets the needs less of a general consumer and more of specific consumption communities. Just at the point when the market dominates society, it fails to provide a sense of collective identity; increasingly, markets identify the differences between us.

A true capitalist market is an unstable force. Marx recognized this in the nineteenth century:

> Constant revolutionizing of production, uninterrupted disturbance of all social conditions, everlasting uncertainty and agitation distinguish the bourgeois epoch from all earlier ones. All fixed, fast-frozen relations, with their train of ancient and venerable prejudices and opinions are swept away, all new-formed ones become antiquated before they can ossify. All that is solid melts into air, all that is holy is profaned.

His words, from *The Communist Manifesto* (1848), have more truth now than when they were written. In the nineteenth century, market relations had to fight against established relations and hierarchies. Religion, state bureaucracies, older cultural norms and sanctions all put limits on a fully functioning capitalism. But at the beginning of the twenty-first century, markets are now the dominant social principle. 'Ancient and venerable prejudices are being swept away'; 'all that is solid melts into air'. The politics of culture is one response to this agitation and uncertainty.

Globalization, as commonly perceived, reinforces this sense of ever-lasting agitation; it feeds into older prejudices of othering. It is a convenient scapegoat. The blame is always out there, on someone else, on them, on it. Globalization gives a name to these fears.

The connection between globalization and nationalism is not clear and simple. Nationalist identity can be reinforced, represented and recreated when a country is undergoing rapid integration into the global economy, or is experiencing quick immersions into global cultural flows and political globalization. In those countries where the connection with the global economy is seen as loss of jobs or large-scale immigration of 'foreigners', cultural politics can take a particularly nasty turn. The rise of racist parties has been reinforced by bigoted hatred of immigrants. Even if they are not electorally successful, racists can wield power by the calculated response of more mainstream parties, who adopt an anti-immigrant stance in order to cut off support to the extremists. While states want an integrated economy, they may also want to strengthen the barriers to immigration. The global economy is an abstract idea, the local immigrant community is a more obvious target for resentment and disquiet.

Globalization is often the name given to the uncertainty and fragmentation of the world of rapid economic change. Just as a spatially homogeneous world reinforces the importance of place, so a perceived globalizing culture may highlight the importance of local culture. But identity is always relational. The identification of 'us' also involves a *non*-'us'. The connection between nationalism and cultural politics raises ugly images: ones in which you can hear a Wagner soundtrack and see images from Leni Riefenstahl. And there are more recent examples that prove the point. The 1990s saw nationalist sentiment reach its ugliest zenith in the Balkans. The break up of the old Yugoslavia and the fallout from Slav and Croatian nationalism created the preconditions for the human tragedy of Bosnia and Kosovo. Genocide, ethnic cleansing, mass rapes. All the old horrors relayed across the world. In this case, however, a political globalization, networks of connections and collective responses provided partial solutions rather than caused the problem. Not in the case of Bosnia, where the Europeans in particular seemed incapable of stopping mass violence, but the NATO response clearly avoided genocide in Kosovo and laid the basis for the overthrow of Milošević and his nationalist gangsters.

Political globalization can also encourage more benign nationalisms. Take Scotland and Wales. Significant nationalist sentiment exists in these two countries. While rarely boiling over into active demands for secession, this form of nationalism has been reinforced by political globalization. The creation of the European Union allows the break-up of the European nation–state. Prior to Britain's linkage with continental Europe's drive for unification, Scottish nationalism was always criticized because it meant loss of connection to a powerful state, the United Kingdom. How could tiny Scotland survive in a world of big powerful states? But now, in the context of a European Union, nationalist sentiments flourish. The European nation–state was always a historical compromise, the result of an incorporation of peripheries by centres in Madrid, Paris and London. The Catalans, Bretons and Welsh can just as easily flourish within a new Europe as they did within the old nation–states. Perhaps even better. Globalization can cause nationalist outbreaks of the worst kind. But more benign nationalism can also flourish in a globalizing world.

The politics of culture takes a number of forms. A globalizing world, and in particular the global discourse of human rights and the creation of world opinion as an important factor in national politics, has paradoxically strengthened the hand of some indigenous groups around the world claiming cultural rights, particularly land rights. The Aborigines in Australia are the indigenous people of an island continent with an occupancy that arguably goes back almost 60,000 years. But since the establishment of the colonial settler society in 1788, they have experienced the same loss as many other indigenous peoples elsewhere in the world. Their land and children were stolen, they were marginalized and oppressed, and even today their living standards and health provisions are much lower than those non-Aborigines enjoy. Life expectancies of Aboriginal people are twenty years less than non-Aborigines. It is not only a story of Aboriginal apathy and white complacency in the face of this institutionalized racism and oppression. On the one hand, there has been intense Aboriginal resistance, and over the past 25 years some major gains have been made. The 1976 Aboriginal Land Rights Act recognized the claims of the indigenous people. Ayer's Rock was given back to its traditional owners, the Anangu, and renamed Uluru. In 1982 three indigenous people – Eddie Mabo, David Passi and James Rice – won a case at Australia's High Court that recognized indigenous land rights. The resultant Native Titles Act of 1993 led to some of the federally owned land being given back to descendants of the traditional owners. In 1993 the Wik people of far-north Queensland also successfully fought a case in the High Court that extended native title to leasehold land. Throughout Australia, Aborigines have reclaimed land and sought to rebuild and strengthen their communities. Many are battling with problems of poor health provision, lack of employment and alcoholism, and there is a long way to go. But to present a picture of Aboriginal apathy is to ignore the truly remarkable resistance, struggle and achievements of Aboriginal Australia. In Alice Springs, where for years Aborigines were banned from restaurants and public spaces, there has been a flowering of Aboriginal tourist businesses and art galleries. In the symbolic centre of Australia there are Aboriginal land holdings, including the Katiti Land Trust and Haast Bluff Land Trust as well as Uluru and Kata Tjuta (formerly The Olgas).

On the other hand, not all non-Aborigines are complacent. Parts of white Australia have also fought for Aboriginal rights. For years the historian Henry Reynolds has been writing popular history books that tell the story from the other side of the frontier. His bestsellers, such as *Blood on The Wattle*, have made today's young Australians acutely aware of the past injustices. The idea of reconciliation has been in the political air for the past decade. This mood was reinforced with the publication of a government report in 1997 that told horrific tales of the separation of Aboriginal children from their families. The report was front-page news and moved the conscience of the country. A National Sorry Day was declared, and, in 1998, over 300 events were held throughout the country. The Governor of New South Wales made a public apology to one of the stolen generation, and thousands of schoolchildren in Sydney wore red, black and yellow in a demonstration of support. Over a million people have signed *Sorry Books* with heartfelt messages of apology and reconciliation. The far-right One Nation Party, which stood on a racist platform of overturning Aboriginal land rights, was roundly defeated in a recent national election.

But behind both movements there was a growing weight of international opinion. Activists could use the sense of Australia's position as a democratic, enlightened country to force action, to shame the public conscience. A global discourse of human rights, an emerging regime of cultural rights and the perceived sense of international public opinion all gave purchase, hope and sustenance to activists. When Sydney hosted the Olympic Games in 2000, activists saw it as an opportunity to make their case, and in the months that led up to the Games, Australians felt obliged to face up to some of the more glaring forms of racial oppression.

Land claims by people around the world are fought in local courts and national arenas, but also in the international court of public opinion. One aspect of globalization is the greater transparency of state governments when dealing with their citizens, especially those who are marginalized. International public opinion works more effectively in some countries than in others, and it is fickle; what was once news becomes taken for granted.

But globalization does not simply overthrow indigenous societies, it can also help to save them from extinction.

Ecological Globalization

Ecological globalization is not new. The Columbian exchange meant a redistribution of peoples, plants and animals that caused lasting changes to ecosystems around the world. Ecological change in the wake of global connections has been occurring for at least 500 years, perhaps for much longer. However, running through the current round of cultural, political and economic globalization is an ecological dimension that is worthy of some discussion. Let us consider three areas: global ecological economics, ecological politics and ecological culture.

Until recently, issues of economic growth and environmental quality were two separate discourses. These two debates not only remained separate; they were often counterpoised one to another. Economic growth was seen as detrimental to environmental protection, while environmental regulation was seen as inhibiting economic growth. Environmental *protection* was contrasted with the need for economic *deregulation*, while *managed* ecosystems were compared to the ideal of *free* trade. To this day the rhetoric of the WTO and the IMF is still dominated by the primacy afforded to free trade. Yet some links have been made. The 1987 UN Brundtland Report, *Our Common Future*, proposed the idea of sustainable development. In principle it means a more mutual relationship between economic growth and environmental protection. In 1992 the UN Conference on Environment and Development, which was attended by more than 100 heads of state, took sustainable development as its organizing principle, and 156 countries signed the Rio Declaration that affirmed the commitment to reconcile trade and environment.

An early test for the Rio Declaration was the negotiations over the

North American Free Trade Agreement (NAFTA). This agreement to link Canada, Mexico and the US was first proposed in 1990 by President Salinas of Mexico. It reached a high level of public interest during the 1992 US Presidential elections. The final agreement was approved by the US Congress in November 1993. What is interesting about the final agreement is the green provision negotiated by both the Bush and Clinton administrations. Environment and labour groups successfully lobbied for a variety of provisions that transformed a simple free-trade agreement into a more complex trade/environmental treaty. Some of the provisions included higher standards on environment regulation and a commitment to upward harmonization, moving towards the highest environmental standards rather than the lowest, and specific plans for the clean-up of the US–Mexico borderlands. A trade agreement between three sovereign countries also included international environmental commitments and treaties such as the 1987 Montreal Protocol on limiting CFCs, the 1973 Convention on endangered species and the 1989 Basel Convention on the transboundary movement of hazardous wastes.[12] There are many criticisms that can be made of NAFTA, but, despite its weaknesses, this was one of the first trade agreements to integrate issues of environmental quality and protection. After NAFTA, environmental concerns, if not quite at the centre of national economic policy, are no longer as far out on the periphery. Free trade had been greened.

The major issue of global ecological economics is how to integrate sustainable development and environmental protection into issues of trade and economic growth. There are still instances where free trade trumps ecological issues. In 1996 the US, under its Endangered Species Act, required shrimp-boats to use nets with turtle excluders. Traditional shrimp-nets killed up to 150,000 sea turtles every year and threatened the species with extinction. Most countries complied with the measure, but India, Malaysia and Pakistan challenged the US measure in the WTO, and the WTO ruled against the US. The sovereign power of a nation–state was undercut by the WTO, which showed a complete lack of environmental sensitivity. The IMF and WTO are still dominated by the ideology of free trade. The issue now facing us is to replace the dominant model of free trade with a more complex model of sustainable development. We need a greening of economic globalization.

An important element in political globalization has been the development of a global ecological politics. Environmental concerns ignore national boundaries. Air pollution drifts across borders, a depleted ozone level affects everyone irrespective of citizenship, and polluted rivers flow from one country to another. Ecological problems do not recognize national sovereignty. Ecological solutions are inherently international. A steadily increasing set of treaties, protocols and conventions has created an international regime of environmental regulation. Examples include the 1973 Convention on Trade in Endangered Species, the 1987 Montreal Ozone Protocol and the 1992 Rio Declaration. The most recent in a long line was the December 1997 meeting in Kyoto, Japan, of over 10,000 government officials and advocacy representatives to discuss climate change. Ten days of negotiations produced the Kyoto Protocol signed by 170 nations that legally committed industrial countries to reduce their emissions of greenhouse gases, especially CO_2, by 5.2 per cent from their 1990 levels by 2008–2012. The commitment is relatively weak since some of the reductions have already happened through the collapse of the former Soviet economy. And some countries, especially the US, is keen to 'trade': the US would buy Russia's lower rate of emissions without undertaking to reduce domestic production. At the time of writing no country has ratified the pact, and the US Congress has both called for less developed countries to have their emissions reduced and baulked at the US ratification. The George W. Bush administration is adamantly opposed to strict air pollution measures. The devil is in the detail. The easy publicity of the initial Kyoto agreement was quickly trumpeted as international cooperation intended to solve a pressing problem. The reality has been recalcitrance, heavy-handed arm-twisting by the US and failure to achieve a global perspective. Domestic politics, especially of the richer countries, is dominating a global issue. The Kyoto Protocol shows that a global environmental regime is more a set of hopes and beginnings than realized policies. At a follow-up meeting in The Hague in November 2000, one environmental campaigner from Canada burned his passport in the Press room. 'Some people think this conference is an exercise in politics, diplomacy and compromise', he said as his passport burst into flames. 'The only thing being compromised is the integrity of the biosphere.'

National environmental policies are now enmeshed in a global regulatory system, in some cases binding, in others more at the level of rhetoric than policy. And power politics play a role, with the biggest polluters able to use their economic and political muscle to dominate the discussions and agreements. But in the course of just 30 years, environmental policy has gone beyond simply a matter for separate states. The global integrity of the biosphere has helped create the beginnings of a global environmental policy. It has been strengthened by a scientific discourse that stresses global perspectives rather the national ones. Science is far more international than politics is. There is a global scientific community, albeit dominated by one language, English, which provides much of the scientific data behind the perception and discussion of ecological issues and environmental problems. But while the scientists have the knowledge, the politicians have the power.

Over the past 35 years the idea of a single earth as an organizing principle has been gaining ground. There has been a growing sense of global integrity and a developing global consciousness. Ecological issues have both embodied and reflected this trend. Technological progress has provided metaphors. In 1966 Kenneth Boulding made the distinction between a 'cowboy economy' and a 'spaceman economy'. A cowboy economy assumes infinite resources, limitless horizons, moving on. A spaceman economy is an environment of limits, fragility and interconnections. A spaceman economy is concerned with husbanding scarce resources, recycling limited supplies and caring for a life-giving environment. The earth is better viewed as a spaceship of finite resources.

Technology also provides compelling images. In 1969 the first photographs of the world from space became available. They showed a beautiful, small round earth shimmering in an inky darkness. The images instantly established themselves as iconic. The earth from space was a complex image. It embodied our technological progress, it revealed a single unit of human occupancy, it showed a single world, a spaceship earth. It is not incidental that on 22 April of the following year, the first Earth Day was celebrated. It provided the context for local activists around the world to celebrate their ecological principles. It was also an opportunity for a party, a celebration and a spectacle. Too much can be read into the increasing size of Earth Day celebrations. For the past 30 years in which they have been celebrated, environmental deterioration has worsened throughout much of the world and levels of consumption continue to increase rather than decrease. While we celebrate a spaceman economy, we are still living in a cowboy one. I once saw someone leave an Earth Day celebration in a monstrous, gas-guzzling, sports-utility vehicle. So much for treading lightly on the earth.

The promise embodied in Earth Day is an important indicator of an ecological consciousness that considers the global as much as the national and the local. Environmentalism, in principle more often than in practice, has become an important way in which we view the world. The environmental movement has had its successes and defeats, but it has become a significant influence with regard to our world view. Environmentalism has become the new global narrative. The greening of consciousness goes along with the globalization of our consciousness. When the world becomes one, then the distinction between here and there falters. There is no empty space then in which to dump toxics, ecological systems are bound together, and environmental health in any one place is dependent on every other place being environmentally healthy. A truly global world is an ecological world.

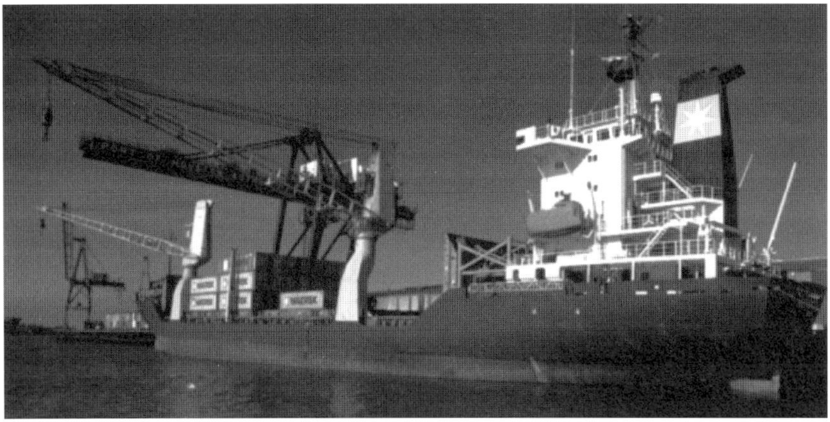

CHAPTER SEVEN

The Annihilation of Space, the Tyranny of Time

Philip II of Spain ruled the first global empire. In 1556 he succeeded to his father's dominions in America and Europe. At its height, his empire included not only great tracts of Europe in Italy, the southern Netherlands and Portugal, but also New Spain (in present-day Mexico), Peru, Brazil and the Spice Islands of South-east Asia. The sun never set on his empire. In order to run it, Philip needed a vast information gathering network. Spies and ambassadors, informants and allies would send reports back to the imperial centre in Castille. Philip had three problems, problems that beset all global networks: space and time, and information overload. Before the invention of the steam engine, human movement was limited to horsepower on land and by wind power on the seas. Distance was overcome, even for the most remote parts of the empire, but at the cost of time. Even within Europe, letters from his ambassadors could take as little as seven days, but, on occasion, as many as 49 days to reach Castille. Messages from the Spanish Netherlands rarely took less than two weeks, while reports from New Spain obviously took much longer. And when the information did arrive, there was too much of it. Information overload was heightened

159

by Philip's determination to read almost all the reports and documents, but even a less hands-on monarch would have had problems. As one historian has noted: 'the delays in communication caused by distance, coupled with the rapid increase in the amount of available data, produced significant confusion in sixteenth-century capitals.[13]

All global networks have to overcome space and time. Indeed, the defeat of these fundamental elements constitutes a global system. We can identify significant relationships between what we can term space–time convergence and globalization. Space–time convergence is the reduction of the time taken to move between places. In 1800 it took a stagecoach almost three and half days to travel from New York to Boston. By 1860 the same distance could be covered in 10 hours by train, and, in 2000, in less than five hours by car, assuming no traffic jams. Transport improvements brought New York and Boston closer together.

In the first phase of globalization, space and time constituted major barriers to global integration. Distance could be overcome, but at a cost. Messages passed slowly and unreliably; information was received late, orders could be delayed. The time taken to cover distance imposed costs. A global economy was possible, but its full elaboration was hampered by distance, time and cost. Places were still far apart from each other.

The second phase of globalization is closely connected to major space–time convergence brought about by the canals, railways and steam-driven ships. These transport improvements reduced the time and hence the cost of sending people, goods and information. We can think of them as compressing space–time: transport improvements bring places closer together in a space–time convergence. Before the opening of the Erie Canal, it could take several weeks to move goods from New York City to upstate towns and cities. When the Canal opened in 1825, the cost of transporting goods was so radically reduced that new goods were put on canal barges. A headline in a newspaper published in upstate Batavia could relish the fact that fresh Long Island oysters were now available. The canal

compressed time and space and hence introduced new commerc
tunities, new connections, a new world.[14] Although the first priv_
company also opened in 1825 – a line connecting Stockton and Darlington
in the North of England – it took some time before the railway became a
dominant form of transport. Construction costs were high, land assembly
was often difficult in congested areas and laying track in sparsely populated tracts was a risk. As with other time–space compressors, there is a
phase in which innovation is only slowly adopted because the benefits are
difficult to foresee or to realize. Once they are, the switch to mass adoption
can be rapid. By 1900 most of the world's cargo was moved by the quicker,
cheaper, more reliable steamships. The resultant space–time convergence
reduced the cost of transporting goods and people around the world.
Between 1870 and 1910 worldwide railway track increased fivefold. The
coming of the railways also transformed many local times into a few standard ones.

Space–time convergence affects not only the economy. It transforms
our view of the world. The railway stations built in Paris became a favourite
subject for the French Impressionist painters. They were recording icons of
the modern world. There is a link between space–time convergence,
modernism and modernity.

The third phase of globalization is marked by even more transport
improvements, and a revolution in the movement of information. The
improvements come in many forms. There are the new forms such as air
transport. The first jet engine flight took place in 1941. Jet engines enabled
planes to travel faster and carry heavier loads. Now the globe is interlaced
with jet flights that carry both people and cargo around the world. The cost
of covering vast distances by jet aircraft has plummeted. Flowers picked in
Colombia can be air freighted to Miami and distributed to stores around
the US before they have time to wilt. This example shows that transport
improvements do not simply reduce existing trade barriers, they help to
manufacture new forms of trade. Jets have created a relatively cheap form

of mass global travel. International tourism and international business has helped create globalization.

Transport modes have also moved on. One of the biggest changes in recent times has been the containerization of goods carried by sea. An important element of economic globalization is the large metal boxes that are freight containers. First developed in 1956, by the late 1960s they had become the standard form of intercontinental transport of goods. Container ships provide a quick and cheap means of transporting goods around the world. Since the late 1980s the cost of shipping has decreased tenfold. In 1990 it cost $30 to ship a VCR; in 2000 it cost just $1.50. When transport costs make up less than one per cent of a retail item's final price, the most important variable becomes labour costs. The global shift in manufacturing has accelerated because once transport costs decline as an absolute and relative proportion of final costs, then labour costs become an even more important variable. When Nike can ship shoes around the world for a fraction of what it costs to produce them, the labour costs of production become a key element in the location of factories.

There has also been a major, albeit unintended, consequence of containerization. In the past 50 years, traditional loading and unloading points at seaports have proved inadequate because of the large amount of land necessary for the bulk storage of containers. Traditional docks could not handle the bulk carriers. Shipping nodes moved closer to the sea, towards cheap, flat land and away from the old urban docklands, which went into rapid decline. However, during the 1980s and '90s many large cities transformed their decayed docks. London's vast Docklands, Baltimore's Inner Harbor and Sydney's Darling Harbour are just three examples of major urban renewal schemes that turned abandoned docks and derelict port facilities into apartments, casinos, restaurants and offices.

The third wave of globalization, the post-1989 one, has been marked by increasing space–time convergence. During the second wave, in 1873,

Jules Verne published his novel *Around the World in Eighty Days*. The title says it all. It was written to show the speed at which an adventurer could travel around the globe. The novel is a series of balloon flights, sea voyages and train-rides. The 80-day circumnavigation was considered a remarkable feat. Now we can travel the world at a fraction of the cost and in a fraction of the time. The cost of covering distance has fallen.

But this third wave is also characterized by a revolution in the transfer of information. In the first wave, in Philip's imperial heyday, information was conveyed in the same way that people and goods were. Messages were hand-delivered, or carried alongside goods and wares for market. Information moved at the same speed as travellers and commodities.

In the second wave of globalization new forms of information technology emerged. The most important was the telegraph. There were early innovators such as Joseph Henry, who in 1831 built an electromagnetic signalling system that consisted of a magnet, energized by electricity, which moved to strike a bell, thus the information was conveyed by coded sound combinations. By 1845, after a full-scale demonstration between Baltimore and Washington, DC, the first telegraph company was formed in the US; the same year the Electric Telegraph Company was formed in England. The first submarine telegraph cable was laid in 1850 between France and England, and the Atlantic cable was successfully laid in 1858, although it did not function properly until 1866. I dated the second wave of globalization from 1865, not only at the close of the Civil War in the US but also at the threshold of an information technology revolution. In the following 60 years a global cable network was established. Information could now travel faster than either people or goods. It was expensive and limits were placed on how much information could be sent. Repeater stations and booster valves were necessary over long distances, and cables had limited capacity. The telegraph transformed business and government, but the high costs meant they tended to be the preserve of government and big business. The British government used the telegraph more than any other country, it was a vital instrument in monitoring its sprawling empire. It was Philip's information-gathering system all over again in Morse code. The telephone was also invented in this second phase of globalization. Alexander Graham Bell patented the telephone in February 1876. The telephone network soon covered the globe. Again, however, costs were prohibitive. Long-distance and international calls were especially expensive. Even as late as 1960 only one in every two households in the US had a telephone, one in eight in the UK and one in seventeen in West Germany. It was not just technology that increased space–time convergence in the second phase of globalization. The global regulatory framework of international cooperation was also important. Traditional forms of information exchange, such as postal services, were improved by international agreements.

The third wave of globalization is intimately connected to the marked space–time convergence brought about by improvements in traditional transport modes. Jet travel, sea transport and cars have all rapidly accelerated space–time convergence. The cost of overcoming space has declined in both real and relative terms. But there has also been a revolution in the transmission of information brought about by microelectronics, the computer and the Internet.

One of the first modern computers was built in 1946 at the University of Pennsylvania. The ENIAC (electronic numerical integrator and calculator) speeded up calculations. The drawbacks were its size and cost. It was nine feet tall, covered about an acre, weighed 30 tons and needed a staff of over 100. The first commercial computers were expensive, bulky and restricted to the military, the largest corporations and well-funded scientific/educational establishments. The computer revolution was not so much the development of the computer as its miniaturization. The first microprocessor, developed in 1971, allowed computers to shrink in size and cost without losing power. The first microcomputer was invented in 1975. From then on the pace of innovation and marketing was rapid: With three partners and a shoestring budget, Apple launched its computers the next year; Apple II was introduced in 1977 and, by 1981, the company had sales of $581 million; in 1981 IBM launched the Personal Computer; Apple's Macintosh was launched in 1984 as a personal friendly computer. The computer revolution was to make computers faster, more powerful, cheaper and smaller. I remember as a graduate student undertaking sophisticated data analysis. I had to punch data cards and carry three trays of them up to a central computer centre. My data limits were determined by the strength of my arms. The cards were fed into a large computer, shared by everyone on the campus, and the results could be picked up three days later. The computer was a huge centralized power system. Ten years later I could do all the calculations at my own desk on my own computer in minutes. Arm strength declined as a limitation on my research.

The Internet was initially developed by the US Defence Department as a communications system that would survive a nuclear attack. It was based on packet-switching communication technology that allowed a horizontal rather than vertical communication; a non-hierarchic form of communication system was less vulnerable than one with key command centres. The first computer network went on line in September 1969 with four nodes at the University of California in Los Angeles, Stanford Research Institute, the University of California in Santa Barbara and the University of Utah. The fully fledged Internet had to await many developments, including protocols of communication that allowed different computers to talk to one another. It also had to await a critical threshold of users. I remember exchanging cards with fellow academics at conferences in the early 1980s, and on their cards would be what I now know to be their email address. But what could I do with it? I did not have email, so their addresses were useless to me. What a stupid thing, I remember thinking. Who will ever use this system? My forecasting skills were about as limited as my computing skills. Globalization requires mass communication usage to be really effective. It is the same with the telephone. Two telephones make a network, but just a few telephones is still a limited system. Only when there is a mass telephone system does the telephone really come into its own. The same with the Internet. In 1990 there were almost no Internet hosts; by 2000 there were 50 million. In 1990 there there no websites, by 2000 there were millions, and I use this loose figure since every day that passes even more are added. The third wave of globalization is causally connected to the revolution in information technology that has allowed the quicker, cheaper, universal transmission of information.

The pace of change in information technology has been staggering. We have a become a wired global network in less than a decade. The speed of the most recent changes has taken us all by surprise. If I had been writing this before the rapid fall of technology stocks from the last quarter of the 2000 I am sure my analysis would have been more optimistic. You can date analysis by which side of this financial fracture line they fall on. Take Manuel Castells's *The Network Society*, a very influential book first published in 1996 with a second edition in 2000. It is overwritten and overawed: information technology as the dawn of the new millennium and the Second Coming, rolled into one with a pinch of California boosterism. It is all new: the new economy, the new society, the new millennium; new technology now replacing the author's former Marxism as the beacon of the future. Technological materialism replacing historical materialism. Writing on the other side of the collapse of the dotcom stock-prices, the new economy looks much like the old economy. The free-wheeling, slightly anarchic computer culture is now being reined in by fiscal discipline and a downturn in investor confidence. When stock-prices for dotcom companies plummet from a high of $143 per share to 9 cents per share, the bubble has definitely burst. When questioned about the meaning and consequences of the French Revolution, the Chinese politician Zhou Enlai (Chou En-lai) replied 'It's too early to tell'. Same with the recent information technology revolution. Too early to tell with any real precision, but in general terms, somewhere between Castells's awestruck, groupie mentality and the very recent, badly shaken market confidence.

Information technology has transformed the globalization of business. Global information is now a key element in any venture, whether it be selling sneakers, trading currencies or mining data sets. Computers have added to the capacity to store, retrieve and analyze this data. Just-in-time production, for example, is impossible to determine without accurate and steady streams of reliable data and forecasts on sales and inventory. Knowledge management and information processing are absolutely vital to contemporary business. I do not subscribe to the sharp distinction made between *new* economy and *old* economy that was made consistently in the late 1990s. Information technology has transformed business, to be sure, but some of the biggest users of this technology are traditional corporations and businesses. The argument that information technology has created a new economy radically different from the old one is an argument that was burned off in the wake of the collapse of technology stock in 2000. Companies such as Yahoo, Ebay and Amazon that could rack up losses with no profits in sight were given a market correction as their stock prices tumbled. The new economy was brought into the old economy. The old/new polarity no longer holds, for traditional companies now rely heavily on information processing, while new economy companies are subject to the same traditional criteria of profit and loss. There is a new economy, but it is an economy that encompasses both new and traditional business; it is an economy in which the availability and analysis of information is generating increased innovation, competition and globalization. Take Ebay and Amazon. They provide information, but they still need to use traditional modes of transport to move their books and auction items. Postal services were invigorated by these two companies, not superseded. Another example: containerization. A container of sneakers made in China is tagged on a computer. The container's path can be followed across the ocean to the docks at Los Angeles. It can then be directed to the regional distribution centres and then to stores where the company's computers have registered an increased demand for their kind of sneakers. The old economy of making and selling sneakers is incorporated into the new economy of rapid information retrieval and analysis. The old economy has utilized the informational economy, which, in turn, uses the goods and services of the old economy. The intermeshing is so complete that it is no longer tenable, in my view, to demarcate meaningfully between old and new economies. In April 2001, Amazon.com agreed to take over Borders.com, the ailing online arm of the bookstore company Borders. This is an example of the new economy and old economy in a partnership that is likely to be the trend of the immediate future, as dotcom companies seek to expand their customer and revenue base and older companies maximize their internet exposure.

Information industries are now a key sector in any advanced economy. Industries involved in the dissemination, creation and management of information are a crucial component of job creation, regional development and urban growth. But as these industries are incorporated into traditional business structures, and as the older industries become more reliant on information processing, it becomes more and more difficult to sustain a dichotomy between old and new economies. The economy has become informationalized and globalized.

The End of Geography?

Many commentators have assumed that rapid space–time convergence is leading to the end of geography. The argument goes like this: space–time convergence has been so rapid and complete that it no longer matters where you are. *The Economist* outlined a future world where,

> instantaneous global telecommunications, TV and computer

networks will soon overthrow the ancient tyrannies of time and space. Companies will need no headquarters, workers will toil as effectively from home, car or beach as they could in the offices that need no longer exist, and events half a world away will be seen, heard and felt with the same immediacy as events across the street – if indeed streets still have any point.[15]

Information technology has promoted many changes: more people can work at home, certain events are broadcast globally. I am not suggesting that the world is unchanged. Rather, I am arguing that recent space–time convergence is making geography more important, not less. The digital revolution is creating new geographies, not replacing geography. The friction of distance has not become the fiction of distance.

The technological changes themselves have been happening in particular places. Technological breakthroughs occur in clusters in both time and space. Centres of innovation, such as Silicon Valley just south of San Francisco, develop where pools of talented people spark off ideas in a risk-taking milieu of available money, information and talent. These centres, once established, generate their own growth as they attract able people and risk capital in a upward cycle of innovation and growth. The very development of space-defeating information technologies is deeply bound up with the particularities of place that foster technological synergy.

The use of information technologies is also uneven. If we measure internet activity by the number of domain names, then studies have convincingly shown that they cluster around metropolitan areas. The city is not so much being replaced by the internet, for the centrality and dominance of certain key cities is being reinforced by it. A close study of the internet and US cities clearly shows that the global cities of New York and Los Angeles contain the largest clusters of internet activity, followed by San Francisco/San Jose and Washington, DC.[16]

Because the internet has increased the amount of information available, it puts a premium on the ability to process this information. A computer terminal now provides a flood of information and data. But it needs to be ordered, surveyed, manipulated, understood and narrated. To do this in real time you need groups of people and institutions that can turn raw information into strategic knowledge. The financial districts of the world are still massively concentrated in large metropolitan areas in order to process the huge amounts of financial data. Space may be defeated, but time still imposes a discipline. In order to monitor huge information flows in real time, it is necessary to have the *information to knowledge* infrastructure of people and institutions; all those spatially concentrated and aggregated resources that allow the rapid processing of information. This infrastructure is unevenly distributed around the world. When we turn space–time coverage from weeks to days and from days to hours, then minutes and seconds become more important. Time is not replaced, it is speeded up, and the places where this *information to knowledge* occur become even more strategically important.

My basic argument is that rapid space–time convergence makes the particularities of place and the efficiency of time even more important. The annihilation of space makes place even more critical. The restructuring of space foregrounds the differences between places. There are examples of the electronic cottage where someone can work from home and still be connected to the outside world. Copy editors, for example, often employed by publishers as contract workers, can do their work and business transactions from home. The growth of the semi-formal sector of the economy in association with telecommunication technologies has allowed some workers to escape the prison of space and move to the place of their choice. But in this smoothed out space–time, place becomes more important in a number of ways. First, while space–time convergence means the freedom from traditional locational pulls, it generates new locational pulls. As transport costs have diminished in relative and absolute terms, other place-specific factors become more important.

Standardized manufacturing processes can now leave old industrial areas and move to cheaper labour areas around the world. Even the standardized information-processing industries now get basic software code and back-office functions done in places like India because of the relatively low labour costs. The installation of reliable high-capacity telephone lines in India and their dedicated workforce has led to more US companies using Indian companies to generate computer code, manipulate data files and even communicate with customers. It is estimated that by 2008 almost a million new jobs and $17 billion in revenue will have been generated, as India becomes a global back office. Second, high-tech industries are moving to places high in amenities. In the post-industrial information sectors of the economy, the locational pull is towards areas that have or can attract high-skilled labour. Even our emblematic copy editors will choose a place based on some locational factors, whether it be close to family, cheap housing, attractive physical location. Third, information-processing sectors such as the financial sector are still attracted to global city locations because of the information to knowledge infrastructures. The continuing dominance of places such as Wall Street, Hollywood and Silicon Valley is testimony to the power of place in the business of information generation and manipulation.

In the increasingly competitive place wars, towns and cities are representing themselves as attractive locations. Place marketing has become an important trend that parallels space–time convergence as places desperately try to catch the next wave of the spatial restructuring.[17]

The rapid changes are generating a massive re-evaluation and devaluation of places. Cities that were once industrial powerhouses can quickly become the black holes of contemporary capitalism; and selected Third World cities are becoming burgeoning industrial centres. In the US, for example, some towns left out by the industrial revolution, such as Austin, Texas, or Madison, Wisconsin, have become favoured high-tech locations. Depending on their location, small towns can either turn into thriving cities or continue their downward spiral.

At both the global and regional levels there has been a transformation of geography.[18] The picture is complex, for old geographies can either be reinforced or undermined at the same time as new geographies are being created. Anthony Townsend's study of US cities and the internet, showed that in terms of domain names and high-capacity internet backbone networks, established global cities such as New York and Los Angeles were important. The new network cities include, in rank order, San Francisco/San Jose, Washington, DC, Boston, Seattle, Miami and Las Vegas. Information black holes include Detroit, Philadelphia, Cleveland and St Louis. The study shows that the urban hierarchy was both being reinforced and restructured as some existing centres, such as New York, maintained their position, while new ones, such as Seattle, were created, and the giants of the metal-bashing era, such as Detroit, were slipping further behind.

Space–time convergence also leads to space–time divergence. Not all places are coming together at the same speed. As some places come closer together faster, then the slower places are effectively witnessing space–time divergence. If we look at the global scale, then while parts of Europe, North America and East Asia have been converging, other parts of the world have been diverging. Much of Africa, for example, is being marginalized as it falls behind in internet, airline and telecommunications connections. Space–time convergence is not experienced equally around the globe; parts of the world are experiencing divergence and resultant marginalization in the global economy.

At the metropolitan level, not all parts of the city are being connected. In the San Francisco/San Jose complex, the poor, minority area of East Palo Alto is, in relative terms, falling further behind in terms of quality of life, income levels and educational standards. To be poor in a booming economy is to become even poorer as housing costs increase. While Washington, DC, is emerging as a well-connected internet city, life in the predominantly black, low-income North-East quadrant of that city continues to be bleak. Even within cities there are differential rates of space–time convergence, just as there are differential rates in the quality of life and connection to the global economy.

Rapid time-space convergence puts a premium on speed. Just-in-Time Delivery. Rapid Response. Quick Turnaround. All mantras that designate a world that is closer together but also speeded up. Even small barriers to this rapid movement of flows are seen as a cost to be overcome or avoided. In the 1980s air freight assured a delivery time within 48 hours of promised time at a specific airport. Now, firms can promise on-time delivery door to door rather than airport to airport. The business has grown enormously as more high-value, time-perishable items are moved around the world. Flowers from Colombia to the US. New England tuna to Japan. The world is increasingly linked by rapid delivery systems. The growing air freight business also reflects frequent changes in fashion that can make late-delivered items perhaps unsellable items. There is an increasing expectation of rapid delivery time.[19]

The minute differences between places in terms of their location within the space of flows become magnified. Space–time convergence does not replace space and time, it exaggerates them. The US headquarters of Federal Express is located in Memphis, Tennessee, because its central time zone location allows the fastest delivery of express mail around the country. When days and hours become more important than weeks and days, then a central location becomes even more important. The placement of Memphis has been revalued in the speeded space of flows that is the US national economy. Other locations have become devalued.

Space–time convergence is apparent in our everyday life. The information technology revolution has been very personal and individual. There has been an emphasis on personal devices, whether they be personal computers, hand-held global positioning systems, videos, mobile phones or laptop computers. Information technology is now a much more integral part of many people's everyday life. Many of us are wedded to the computer screen and hooked to our cellphones. These links have created new forms of globalization. More of the world is 'available' to us as individuals, subject to our personal gaze. With a small computer and an internet hook-up, you can surf the web, check out weather in Australia, buy and sell stocks, peruse the contents of the Library of Congress. Our connection to the world has been deeply changed; what was once distant and far has become close and accessible.

There has been a profound transformation in the subtle connections between the wired society, national communities and individual identity. The new information technology and rapid space–time convergence has collapsed the old connection between community and place. When transport and communications are difficult and expensive, community is more a function of place. Our friends and connections are local, face to face, rooted in the locale. For many poor people in the rural parts of the world, this is still the reality of their lives. For others, especially in the richer countries of the world, community can become more elastic. For individuals, this can mean the virtual communities of chat-rooms and bulletin boards. Communication no longer needs to be face to face or via voice; it can become a cyber-connection that raises issues of the fluidity of identity. A 1993 *New Yorker* cartoon showed two dogs in front of a computer screen, with one dog saying to the other 'On the internet, nobody knows you're a dog'. Anonymous chat-rooms allow us to transcend the limitations of self. But the collective self can be reinforced as diasporas are increasingly linked by the availability of cheap flights, videos, faxes and email that allow old identities to be maintained in new places. Around the world, expatriate communities are maintained by regular links with home that include return travel, visits from relatives, the quick transmission of news, goods and services. There is an interesting globalization/localization nexus as globalization means more people live away from home, but globalization also means that the connections between home and not-home are strengthened. Globalization reinforces the local, just as the local is being restructured by the global. Expatriate communities can become more linked to home, and, in turn, home becomes more globalized as migrants can more easily send back money, information, ideas, goods and services. We should replace the notion of community as a place-bound centre with the image of community as network of global flows that both undermine and reinforce the local.

Personal identity is less constrained by the hard boundaries of a restricted space. When we can move about easily, and draw on ideas, images and inspiration from a global range of sources, personal identity can become more fluid – less a fixed static node and more an assemblage of flows. There has been both softening of identity, as some of us today are able to draw on a wider range of sources of meaning, but there has also been a hardening, as fundamentalist ideologies of various stripes take on an attractive certainty for many people living in what they perceive as a world in flux, a space of flows. Choice and diversity can be threatening to many people, who replace them with certainties. Religious fundamentalism is less a return to the past, more a response to a globalized present.

The disconnection between community and place is most apparent at the regional and national levels, where differential space–time convergence and global connectivity is creating very dissimilar experiences within the same city and same country. Those doing well out the global connection have seen their incomes increase substantially, while those left behind have seen a relative decline in wages. Office workers in India churning out computer code for a sleeping US market can earn from $1,600 to $2,100 a year. Low by Western standards, but a fortune by Indian ones. The city and the nation were always unequal communities, but it has become more pronounced as some have forged ahead and others have been left far behind. The separation is made solid in the rise of gated communities and the politics of exclusion. Growing urban, regional and national inequality is creating a dangerous level of resentment, anger and frustration as the community of city and nation become riven with rising inequality. The digital divide and the flip side space–time convergence are creating a more unequal world. A new geography of inequality is being formed that is undermining civic and national communities.

Even when conquering space we are still left with the tyranny of time. As the world has speeded up, time has not been defeated, it has been magnified. Just-in-Time Production. Immediate Delivery. Next Day Service. Our world has become a place where days have replaced weeks, and hours have replaced days. With space–time convergence, more distance is expected to be travelled in the same time, more work is required. Time is now broken down into increasingly valuable, increasingly smaller units. The effects on our personal lives have been dramatic. Futuristic reports written in the 1960s and 1970s discussed the problem of increased leisure time. New labour-saving devices would free up more time. What would we do with this 'extra' time was a recurring question for the social analysts of only 30 years ago. Labour-saving devices have increased, but the savings have been offset by the increasing value of time. We are working longer and harder. Multi-tasking is the order of the day. We drive and talk business on our cellphones at the same time.

Time-saving devices have reinforced the tyranny of time. With rapid space–time convergence, smaller units of time become more valuable. There has been a marked time compression. As Robert Reich has noted in *The Future of Success* (2001), 'steady' jobs have disappeared into a polarization of fast-track and slow-track jobs. If you are on the fast track, time is too valuable for it to be 'wasted' on other things. Those on the fast track have less time to spend on family and civic affairs as work crowds out other things. We no longer have steady jobs; we have fast-track and slow-track jobs, an inequality reflected in conditions of employment.

Time compression is evident, not just in the supercharged economy, but also the the pace of our everyday life. I see more people driving while speaking into cellphones, sipping coffee while working on screen, talking on the telephone as they surf the web. We are packing more and more into smaller units of time. We are overworked, harried, anxious. Look at people driving on the roads: people are so highly geared that seconds seem like years. No wonder road rage is increasing. As computers get faster, the seconds it takes to log on seem increasingly longer. We are in a frenzied dance with time. There is now a politics of time. We need to reclaim our composure, take time off and spend it with friends, family, children. In a speeded-up world, the struggle against time is the battle to reclaim our civic life, family connections and personal peace of mind.

Those on the connected side of the digital divide are like Philip of Spain. He had a stream of information directed at him from all over the world. We are even luckier than Philip, since space–time convergence has conquered distance. What took weeks and days now takes hours and minutes. We have solved one of Philip's problems. We have annihilated space. But the tyranny of time and the avalanche of information that threaten to choke us still persists. We do not have enough time to look at all the information, connect with all the possible flows. As it was for Philip, there is still the enduring problem of how to transform information into knowledge. But there are differences between then and now. The third wave of globalization is marked by rapid space–time convergence. Space and time have become more important, not less. There are new geographies of place re-evaluation and devaluation, emerging politics of time, the increasing importance of place and a rupturing of traditional connections between community and self, and space and place.

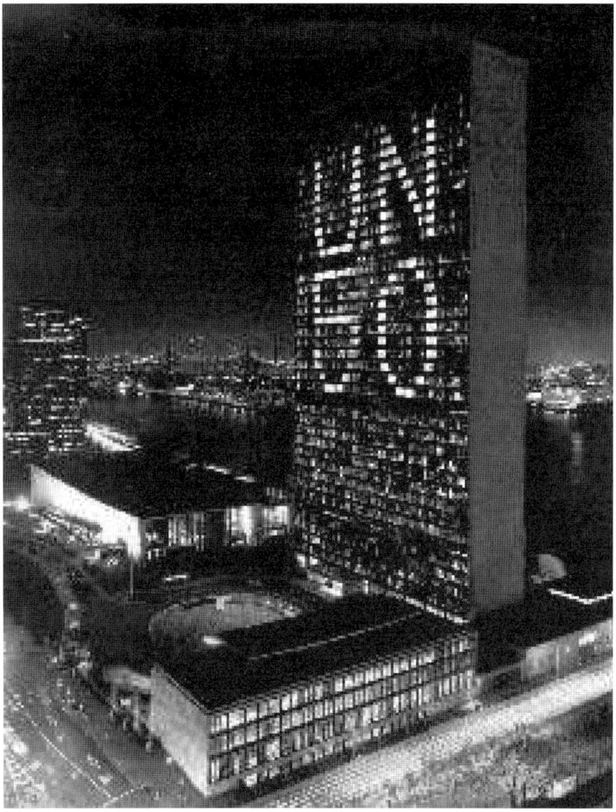
UN
50

CHAPTER EIGHT

Democratizing Globalization

Globalization is entering a new and important phase. The third wave of globalization that began in 1989 has been dominated by three things: the power of the rich countries, such as the US, to set the agenda of global governance; the power of international bureaucracies to operate global governance without democratic consultation; and the power of multinationals, banks and financial institutions to dominate the pace, direction and consequences of globalization.

It is easy to understand how one popular response has been a blanket condemnation of globalization and the emergence of an anti-globalization lobby that looks forward to the overthrow of such institutions as the WTO and IMF and a reversal of global integration. Corporate and bureaucratic interests have dominated the globalization process. But rather than condemn globalization, we need to imagine what a humane globalization would look like. What would a democratic, equitable, ecological globalization look like? What form could it take? What beliefs and myths would it call upon?

The problem is not globalization, but the limited range of narratives that it incorporates. Globalization embodies the power of the rich, the connected and the corporate. Globalization has been dominated by those that fly business class. The rest of us are either back in coach, overcrowded, badly fed and cramped, or worse, not even on the plane, simply stuck in some field somewhere looking up at transcontinental jets flying 30,000 feet above our heads. Those in business class have been kept separate, able to espouse an ideology of free markets, privatization, the bottom line, the Get-with-the-Programme-or-Fail babble of macho monetarism and testosterone capitalism. The global has been the adjective of choice for those eager to discipline labour, undermine ecological standards, move towards a market where labour has less power and nation–states have limitations placed on their ability to regulate markets for the social good. But what would other types of globalization look like?

To begin, we need to foster an international civil society that works towards ensuring social justice and acts as a counterweight to the voices of the business class. We need new narratives, original ideas and sustaining myths to create a global civil society that encompasses cultural diversity and promotes economic equity. But how do we internationalize politics and embrace diversity, given the enduring socializing power of the nation–state? The other side has an easier time; their mantra is clear and simple: privatization, free trade, open markets, global economy. But how about alternative slogans of democratization, fair trade, responsible markets, global society?

The time has come for democratic social movements to both think and act global. There have been progressive examples. Recent years have seen a global democracy movement as people around the world have successfully changed their political circumstances – the people-power of the Philippines, the collapse of Communist power in Europe, the overthrow of Milošević in Yugoslavia in October 2000. There have been setbacks, but global public opinion has been a positive force, giving support and succour to opposition movements in dangerous circumstances.

One of the best hopes for a more humane globalization is to promote the idea of global citizenship and global democracy. The last 300 years has seen, in both theory and practice, a codification of the principles of democratic citizenship in the nation–state. We need to focus as much attention on the global scale. But how can we be global citizens? What would principles of global democracy look like? How can we connect universal principles to local and national circumstance without undermining creative difference and healthy heterogeneity and allowing unjust practices to continue simply because they are part of local and national traditions? If a nation has a tradition, a policy that limits the role of women in society, should we tolerate that as a mark of cultural difference or should we seek to impose universal principles, all the while remembering that the 'universal' tends to be Western liberal values? Despite the problems, I would subscribe to a project of developing universal principles even though there are traces of Western intellectual imperialism. I think the core values are capable of wider appeal and development.

Then there are practical matters. Nation–states have traditions, networks and institutions that foster engagement and empowerment of ordinary citizens in various and varying degrees. Voting and elections can be fixed but at least they allow, if more often in the form rather than the reality, citizen engagement and empowerment. But how can this operate at the global level? A start has been made by the demonstrations against the IMF, World Bank and WTO. These demonstrations have successfully brought wider attention to these previously shadowy centres of global governance. More sustained pressure will promote a democratization of these institutions so that they become more open, more susceptible to popular accountability.

It is one of those times in human history when we need new ideas. I am acutely aware that this chapter is full of questions and precious few answers. We desperately need new ideologies and tactics that connect governments, non-government organizations, progressive social movements and ordinary citizens. How do we connect across global space the many people and organizations that are deeply rooted in place across space?

We need to develop ideas and practices of the global village as well as the global economy, global citizenship as well as national citizenship, global democracy as well as global market, global justice as well as global economic growth, engagement and empowerment as well as production and consumption.

In the last 200 years most progressive movements have concentrated on the nation–state. And rightly so. This was the main level of power, the commanding height where political power was concentrated. Levers could be found and switched, progressive policies were generated. In the new millennium the state is still hugely powerful. I have shown that globalization can indeed strengthen the state, not just undermine it. But we need an internationalization of the progressive movements so that local, national and global are more fully integrated into coherent strategies of reform and social progress. The choice is not between national citizenship and global citizenship. Both are possible. At the moment, national citizenship contains both obligations and rights, whereas global citizenship has, as yet, very little of either. The UN Declaration of Human Rights is a beginning, but the obligations of global citizenship still need to be developed. There is a huge asymmetry between national and global citizenship. One is legally defined, the other more in the process of becoming than being. The old distinction of nationalist or internationalist, local or cosmopolitan, is no longer a stark choice. It is not only possible to be both; it is now essential.

There are enormous difficulties in such a project. There are questions of agendas and tactics. There is also one of motivation. People are wary. The Communist movement, the hope of so many at the beginning of the twentieth century, had become, by the end of that century, an outdated ideology, a failed dream, a lost cause. And even Socialism had become sullied and largely abandoned. Repeating these old mantras will condemn us to political oblivion. We need to capture the central themes of democratic accountability, social justice, ecological sustainability, citizen empowerment, civil engagement and global equity in forms that can appeal to, and galvanize, people. There is a great hunger in the world. Not only for the basic nutritional necessities, but for new stories, new sustaining visions, new ideas of what our world should look like and should become. There is widespread dissatisfaction with the one-dimensional, unfulfilling promise of a corporate globalization. We need a new vision of a humane, democratic and fair globalization.

We need to shift the debate about globalization away from its narrow focus on trade, investment, property rights and capital to include democracy, cultural diversity, workers rights, social justice and environmental sustainability. We need an international Bill of Rights to secure workers' rights, ecological standards and political freedoms. A huge task. But if globalization is to be anything more than corporate globalization devoted to a single borderless economy, we need to imagine what a democratic globalization could be like, envision a humane globalization centred on an international civil society that can operate between formal politics and corporate interests. Globalization has taken the form it has because an international civil society has been slow to develop, outflanked and outrun by government bureaucracies and corporate interests. We urgently need a democratic, ecologically sensitive, fair globalization. It is a struggle of epic proportions. The prize is nothing less than the shape of world geography, the direction of human history and the fate of the entire world.

References

1 We should be very wary of seeing cultural globalization as a recent phenomenon. The counter case was presented at a Metropolitan Museum exhibition entitled 'Year One', which showed evidence of cultural mixing throughout the eastern hemisphere over 2,000 ago. See E. J. Milleckeer, ed., *The Year One: Art of the Ancient World East and West*, Metropolitan Museum of Art (New York, 2000).
2 For silver in particular, see Joyce Jensen, 'Silver and World Trade', *The New York Times* (2 December 2000), p. B13.
3 Paul Kennedy, *The Rise and Fall of the Great Powers: Economic Change and Military Conflict from 1500 to 2000* (New York, 1987).
4 Kennedy, *Rise and Fall*, p. 48. Kennedy goes on to note that 'At the centre of the Spanish decline . . . was the failure to recognize the importance of preserving the economic underpinnings of a powerful military machine' (p. 50).
5 J. A. Hobson, *Imperialism: A Study* (3rd edn, London, 1938).
6 See the revealing article by William Finnegan, 'After Seattle: Anarchists get Organized', *The New Yorker* (17 April 2000), pp. 40–54.
7 *Journal of Commerce* (7 December 1999), p. 1.
8 Quoted in Robert Block, 'How Big Mac survived NATO's attack on Yugoslavia',

Herald American (5 September 1999), pp. E1–E3.
9   Arjun Appadurai, *Modernity at Large: Cultural Dimensions of Globalization* (Minneapolis, 1996), p. 109.
10 This account of English, geography and journals is drawn from a research paper by J. R. Short, A. Boniche, Y. Kim and P. Li, 'Cultural Globalization, Global English and Geography Journals', *Professional Geographer*, 53 (2001), pp. 1–11.
11 Joe Klein, 'Eight Years', *The New Yorker* (16 and 23 October 2000), pp. 188–217 (200).
12 This topic is examined in greater detail in L. M. Benton and J. R. Short, *Environmental Discourse and Practice* (Oxford, 1999), chap. 10.
13 Geoffrey Parker, *The Grand Strategy of Philip II* (New Haven, CT, 1998), p. 289.
14 Carol Shields, *The Artificial River: The Erie Canal and the Paradox of Progress, 1817–1862* (New York, 1996).
15 'Does it Matter Where you Are?', *The Economist* (30 July 1994), p. 13.
16 Anthony Townsend, 'The Internet and The Rise of The New Network Cities, 1969–1999', *Environment and Planning Bulletin*, 28 (2001), pp. 39–58.
17 See my 'Urban Imagineers, Boosterism and The Representation of Cities', in Andrew Jonas and David Wilson, eds, *The Urban Growth Machine* (Albany, NY, 1999).
18 Joel Kotkin has written of the new geography emerging from the digital revolution in his *The New Geography* (New York, 2000).
19 Barry Lopez spent months travelling on air freight 747s around the world; his essay 'Flight' makes fascinating reading. See Barry Lopez, *About this Life* (New York, 1998).

Select Bibliography

Appadurai, Arjun, *Modernity at Large: Cultural Dimensions of Globalization* (Minneapolis, 1996)
Barber, Benjamin, *Jihad vs. McWorld* (New York, 1995)
Benyon, John and David Dunkerly, eds, *Globalization* (New York, 2001)
Castells, Manuel, *The Rise of The Network Society* (2nd edn, Oxford, 2000)
Cox, Kevin, ed., *Spaces of Globalization: Reasserting the Power of the Local* (New York, 1997)
Crystal, David, *English as a Global Language* (Cambridge, 1997)
Held, David and Anthony McGrew, David Goldblatt and Jonathan Perraton, *Global Transformations* (Stanford, CA, 1999)
Friedman, Thomas, *The Lexus and the Olive Tree: Understanding Globalization* (New York, 1999)
Grant, Richard and John Rennie Short, eds, *Globalization at the Margins* (Basingstoke, 2001)
Hiaasen, Carl, *Team Rodent: How Disney Devours The World* (New York, 1997)
Hirst, Paul and Graham Thompson, *Globalization in Question* (Cambridge, 1996)
Hutton, William and Anthony Giddens, eds, *Global Capitalism* (New York, 2000)
Iyer, Pico, *The Global Soul: Jet Lag, Shopping Malls and The Search for Home* (New

York, 2000)
Jameson, Fredric and Masao Miyoshi, eds, *The Cultures of Globalization* (Durham, NC, and London, 1998)
Kachru, Braj, *The Alchemy of English* (Chicago, 1990)
Kapstein, Ethan, *Sharing The Wealth: Workers and the World Economy* (New York, 2000)
King, Anthony, ed., *Culture, Globalization and the World-System: Contemporary Conditions for the Representation of Identity* (Minneapolis, 1997)
Lechner, Frank and John Boll, eds, *The Globalization Reader* (Oxford, 1999)
Micklethwait, John and Adrian Wooldridge, *A Future Perfect: The Challenge and Hidden Promise of Globalization* (New York, 2000)
Mosler, David, *Global America* (Westport, CT, 2000)
Ohmae, Kenicihi, *The Borderless World* (revd edn, New York, 1999)
Reich, Robert, *The Future of Success* (New York, 2001)
Robertson, Roland, *Globalization: Social Theory and Global Culture* (London, 1992)
Sassen, Saskia, *The Global City: New York, London, Tokyo* (Princeton, NJ, 1991)
—, *Losing Control? Sovereignty in the Age of Globalization* (New York, 1996)
Sen, Amarta, *Development as Freedom* (New York, 1999)
Short, John Rennie, *New Worlds, New Geographies* (Syracuse, NY, 1998)
— and Yeong-Hyun Kim, *Globalization and the City* (Harlow, 1999)
Sklair, Leslie, *The Transnational Business Class* (Oxford, 2000)
Tomlinson, John, *Globalization and Culture* (Chicago, 2000)

Acknowledgements

I owe a debt to three people. Barry Bullen expressed enormous confidence in me. He suggested I write this book. Michael Leaman promoted the enterprise and showed a great deal of trust.

This book was written for many reasons. At the obvious level, I thought globalization was an important issue that deserved an airing. As a geographer I have a particular concern with space, place and generating an understanding of the environment around us. The term *geography*, after all, derives from the idea of writing about the world. I felt that much of the writing on globalization was either too academic or too journalistic. I have nothing against either. I am an academic, and for a long time had fantasies of being a journalist. I use these terms as adjectives to refer to esoteric texts or superficial treatments. I have strived for some middle ground. It is a difficult place to reach.

I owe my biggest debt to Lisa. She lived with this writing project. It took up much time and much energy. It is a paltry recompense to dedicate this book to her.

List of Illustrations

Cover: Long Island, Manhattan Island, metropolitan New York City and the lower Hudson River valley, photographed from space, May 1991. Photo: NASA/National Space Science Data Center (NSSDC).

p. 6: Earth, as seen from the Apollo 10 spacecraft, 185,000 km on the way to the moon, May 1969. Photo: NASA/National Space Science Data Center (NSSDC).

p. 20: Millennium Night fireworks in Sydney. Photo courtesy of Tourism New South Wales, Australia.

p. 50: Tear-gas bombardment during demonstrations at the Seattle WTO trade liberalization talks, 30 November 1999. Photo: Bill Stender.

p. 86: A Nike factory in Jiaozhou City, Shandong, China.

p. 114: A Teriyaki McBurger™ in a McDonald's restaurant in Japan. Photo: Daniel Laursen (www.daninjapan.com).

p. 134: An aerial view of Madison, Wisconsin, showing the smoke-stacks of Madison's electricity-generating plant.

p. 158: A container ship in the Panama Canal.

p. 178: The UN headquarters in New York, on the UN's 50th anniversary in 1995.